AMERICAN
Culture
A SAUDI ARABIAN PERSPECTIVE
and Religious Diversity

written by:

FAHAD A. ALHOMOUDI, Ph.D.

edited by:

REBECCA K. MAYS

foreword by:

James B. Smith

UNITED STATES AMBASSADOR TO THE KINGDOM OF SAUDI ARABIA

WESTERN STUDIES INSTITUTE
ECUMENICAL PRESS

Distributed by Temple University Press

written by

FAHAD A. ALHOMOUDI, Ph.D. :: *Western Studies Institute*
Imam Muhammad bin Saud Islamic University
Princess Nora bint Abdul Rahman University, Consultant

edited by

REBECCA K. MAYS
M.A. University of Pennsylvania
Project Director, The Dialogue Institute, Temple University

First published in the United States of America by
the Western Studies Institute and the Ecumenical Press,
Temple University, 1114 W. Berks St., Philadelphia, PA
19122-6090.

Telephone :: *215-204-7714*

Fax :: *215-204-4569*

Website :: *www.westernstudiesinstitute.org*
www.jesdialogue.org

ISBN :: 0-931214-13-0

DISTRIBUTED BY :: *Temple University Press*

book design and art direction

ULLMAN DESIGN :: *www.ullmandesign.com*

Contents

CULTURE :: RELIGION :: POLITICS :: IDEAS ::
EXPERIENCES :: KNOWLEDGE :: COMMUNITY
UNDERSTANDING :: SUPPORT :: FRIENDSHIP ::
SCHOLARSHIP :: COLLABORATION :: PERSPECTIVE

4

Dedication

King Abdullah Bin Abdulaziz

I would like to dedicate this book to King Abdullah Bin Abdulaziz, Custodian of the Two Holy Mosques.

The experiences that I had as a participant in the U.S. Fulbright Interfaith Action Program would not have been possible without King Abdullah's Interfaith Dialogue Initiative which inspired and encouraged me to engage in interfaith dialogue and practical activities toward peace.

It is my sincere hope that this record of my journey will inspire others to reap the benefits of engaging with people of other faiths to help create harmonious coexistence and peace in our world.

by Fahad A. Alhomoudi, Ph.D. {

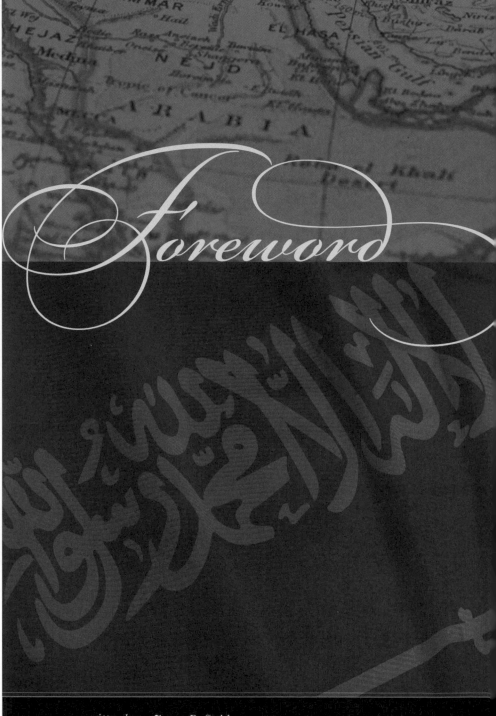

Foreword

written by: **James B. Smith**

UNITED STATES AMBASSADOR TO THE KINGDOM OF SAUDI ARABIA

} One of my great pleasures as United States Ambassador to the Kingdom of Saudi Arabia is to engage in a daily exchange of ideas with people from all walks of life here in the Kingdom. The experience gives life to the many hours of study in advance of the assignment here, and the personal interaction provides for a much richer insight into the country, its citizens, their culture, and tradition.

For many years, American institutions of higher education and the United States government have studied the cultural intricacies of other nations, including Saudi Arabia. This book represents a different approach. By sharing his experiences and insights as a participant in the 2008 U.S. Fulbright Interfaith Action Program (ICAP), Dr. Alhomoudi has given us a rare, substantive account of the historical development of faith communities in the United States and how they compare to the structure of society and beliefs of people in the Muslim World. It is through the exchange of ideas, like the dialogues stimulated by the Fulbright ICAP Program, that a richer, deeper understanding and respect can continue to evolve.

I was especially impressed by the way the author invites the reader to be his companion on this journey, using humorous anecdotes, excerpts from passionate discussions, and concise, but profound descriptions of historical events that have deeply affected our societies and the world. The succinct interpretations of the various religions that exist in America are only a small portion of the value of this publication. Dr. Alhomoudi shows, through his own cultural observations and the personal experiences of participants, presenters, and new-found friends, that theory and practice may be sisters, but they certainly are not twins. He digs deeper to reveal 'how' and 'why' certain shifts in religious and secular beliefs have occurred and explains their qualities from his Saudi world-traveler point-of-view.

Through King Abdullah's initiative with the National Dialogue, Saudi Arabia has undertaken a national initiative to reexamine faith, family and education. It represents an important initiative for dialogue between our two nations and among the nations of the world. Dr. Alhomoudi has made an important contribution in the same spirit, and I hope that it serves as a catalyst for much more discussion as we strive to understand ourselves and our cultures, enriching the way we relate to one another, as individuals and nations.

8

This book addresses the grassroots of two nations, known for their long friendship and collaboration, Saudi Arabia and the United States of America.

Preface

} Current misunderstandings, however, are creating a distance between these two nations. My intention in writing this book is to build a bridge to open a channel for dialogue among American and Saudi people.

Three perspectives shape the style of this book. First, I use a descriptive lens to present what I have seen or experienced during my stay in the U.S. In the second perspective, I provide an informative summary of what I have come across of the people, historical sites, religious places, and concepts. And in the third perspective, through reflection, I interpret what I have seen or learned, including many of the intellectual discussions I had with the other ICAP members and Americans I met during my journey. Where I give information, I consulted friends, did my own research, and received help from research assistants. In some cases friends or assistants contributed paragraphs of their own that I have incorporated. A book like this requires ongoing modification and I invite readers to engage with the interpretations here for that purpose. For now I choose to publish it at this stage with the intention of a writing a second edition that will include the influence of reader responses and further research.

10

Acknowledgments

} First, I would like to express my deepest appreciation and gratitude to His Royal Highness King Abdullah bin Abdulaziz Al Saud of Saudi Arabia for providing Saudi Arabia and its citizens with an opportunity to lead world change through his global initiatives for peace and dialogue.

I would also like to thank the Fulbright Program as well as the staff members of the Council for International Exchange of Scholars, especially Sabine O'Hara, for nominating me as a Fulbright Visiting Scholar, which led to writing this book, and for their unfailing support during my stay in the USA. My gratitude extends to the faculty and staff of the Dialogue Institute at Temple University, especially to Professor Leonard Swidler. My thanks also extend to the entire staff and faculty of the Theology Department at Loyola University, particularly my host Professor William French. Also, I would like to thank my two research assistants at Loyola University Adam Hankins and William Myatt.

During my stay in America, I met a great many friends who made me feel at home. I cannot list them all, but I would at least like to mention Aana Vigen, Marcia Hermansen Carl and Pecki Witonsky. Few words can describe my debt to Rebecca Mays who meticulously edited my book and my appreciation extends to her family for their dedication and friendship. Likewise, my thanks extend to Natalie Komitsky for proofreading the final draft of this book.

I would also like to express my thanks to Sulaiman Aba Alkhail, the Rector of Imam Muhammad ibn Saud Islamic University for his unfailing support. Additionally, I would like to thank Her Highness Princess Al-Joharah Al-Saud, the Rector of Princess Noura bint Abdulrahman University, for her continuous encouragement and support.

As the last paragraph is customarily reserved for expressing the greatest debt and the highest gratitude, I thank first my parents for their love, endless support, and guidance. And then I thank my wife Sara and my children Abdulaziz, Muhammad, Nouf and Abdulrahman who provided me with the most significant source of support throughout my journey. Their generous understanding and compassion have been constant.

11

Introduction

Prayer and travel both require the courage to open to journeys of discovery. Fortuitous intersections of chance meetings among people guide the way. This book is the result of these two kinds of journeys and the friendships formed.

written by: Rebecca K. Mays

DIALOGUE INSTITUTE, TEMPLE UNIVERSITY

} In the fall of 2008, ten Fulbright scholars met at The Dialogue Institute at Temple University in Philadelphia for their three-week orientation to religious pluralism in the U.S. They came from France, Malaysia, Indonesia, Africa, England, India, Israel, Pakistan, Lebanon, and Saudi Arabia. As a graduate student of religious studies with a focus on interreligious dialogue, I was beginning a fellowship with The Dialogue Institute to work with this group and others to build skills in doing interfaith dialogue. These Fulbright scholars earned their grants for the caliber of study and interfaith activities each one pursues in his or her home region. Now, based on that work, each would go to a different American campus for three months to study, teach about their own work, and learn of the American interfaith initiatives. The mood during the orientation was cooperative, even joyful, with each person hopeful and ready to engage.

Dr. Fahad Alhomoudi, a professor of Islamic Law at Imam Muhammad bin Saud Islamic University in Saudi Arabia, kept a journal of his three-month sojourn in Philadelphia and Loyola University in Chicago, Illinois. With a Ph.D. from McGill University in Montreal, Canada (2002-2006), and having worked in academic institutions in the USA (1997-2001), Dr. Alhomoudi hoped to write about his continuing experience with western universities and American culture. As an accomplished scholar, he thought first to do a scholarly article, but the anecdotal journal allowed him more freedom to record contemporary American religion and life as well as describe friendships formed. American readers are even likely to learn of their own cultural and religious history given his research into subjects we often take for granted. This book is the fruit of his study and journal-keeping; he hopes for reader responses that will help him make it even more accurate and useful for an Arabic version that will circulate in Saudi Arabia.

Given the many cultural differences between us, I have erred as editor in the direction of Dr. Alhomoudi's style of English, changing only enough to be readable for the general American reader in order not to lose some of the freshness of his

perceptions. His facility for religious understanding and keen cultural observation are invitations to a valuable Saudi and American exchange. His and my friendship, forged in the course of this project, was itself an example of the dialogue interfaith activism wants to support.

Respect and a willingness to learn are the keys to good dialogue. I met my first Muslim family when I was a young teacher and the class wanted Basima Ahed to take the lead role in a play we were producing. As a devout Muslim family, the parents did not want Basima to do the acting as it might not be a faithful adherence to the Islamic injunction that graven images, idols, or representations of people cannot stand in the place of one's surrender to God. I wanted to be respectful of this constraint and was ready to choose a different actress when certain members of the class volunteered to visit and to dialogue with the parents. I trusted the students to know better what was needed and said I would support whatever the parents chose. They chose to allow their young high school daughter to play the role. She was superb and the entire family who came to watch were very proud. I was sensitive to both their joy and to the constraint that questioned whether participation was appropriate.

Now decades later I am even more sensitive to the need for respect for a devout faith at the same time the need to participate in international affairs pulls Muslims onto the socioeconomic and political world stage. We are now a global neighborhood and face many common problems that cross the lines of traditional faith boundaries. For example, is the rise of interest in hip-hop in North Africa in the best interest of the next generation? Will dietary laws influence food marketing? How will Muslims who do not lend money for interest reconcile their practices with the banking industry? And what does gender equity look like that is still faithful to God? As Muslims come to terms with the influences of modernity and global interdependencies, I as an American interfaith activist want to learn how my assumptions about what is appropriate and ethical might need to evolve. The movement of people of differing faiths from country to country is changing the ways we each live. The task, then, is to be able to learn how to respect one another and to dialogue about those differences that could lead to unnecessary violence and misunderstanding. This journal of observations and insights is intended to help build this respect and encourage the necessary dialogue. Dr. Fahad Alhomoudi has accepted King Abdullah's initiative to start a global Dialogue of Civilizations and is taking steps to make that dialogue productive.

Under the patronage of King Abdullah bin Abdulaziz, the Custodian of the Two Holy Mosques, the Muslim World League held a global interfaith conference in Madrid, Spain, July 16-18, 2008. Nearly 300 religious, political, and cultural leaders from 50 different countries met in a shared purpose Saudi King Abdullah articulated: "If we want this historic encounter to succeed, we must look to the things that unite us; our profound faith in God, the noble principles and elevated ethics that represent the foundation of religions." One of the objectives of the conference was to call upon the UN General Assembly to conduct a special UN session on dialogue with the King and selected others present; that session happened in November, 2008. As the world becomes a single space local interpretations of religion and culture will inevitably be challenged. The King has recognized the challenge and is inviting the dialogue necessary to meet it.

In Dr. Alhomoudi's and my dialogue, a key element of Islam has helped make a bridge for discussion and learning. As a Christian/Quaker I trust that God unifies the understandings of people who work toward the common good. The Islamic concept of *tawhid* meaning "unity" sounds similar to me. Muslims believe that the Qur'an is divine revelation given to the prophet Muhammed in the seventh century. Imams, scholars, and lay practitioners memorize, chant, and interpret this sacred text on behalf of God's *tawhid*. This unity or the complete trust in only one God as transcendent is at the core of religious experience as a Muslim. The *shahadah* or Muslim confession of faith asserts: "There is no God but God." Neither graven images nor idols nor associations nor saints can stand in the place of this experience of surrender to the *tawhid* of God.

Consequences of this trust in a transcendent God then influence assumptions about what it means to be human. The primary purpose of human beings is to fulfill God's unity on earth, in full freedom to choose to do good and to avoid evil. Following divine will is imperative and is the reason for *tafsir*, exegesis of scripture, and *shariah*, the laws or imperatives based on the knowledge of God's unity. A central assumption about being human is that each person regardless of religious historical tradition has an innate capacity for apprehending *tawhid*. Islam names this capacity *din al-fitrah* or natural religion. These understandings about apprehension of God, the freedom as humans to exercise moral choices, and our innate capacity for following divine will together lay the strong foundation for dialogue among believers around the globe.

Dr. Alhomoudi and I will differ on many outward practices and theological concepts as Sunni Muslim and Quaker Christian. But we have experienced in our dialogue what in each of our traditions demonstrates for us the worth of the risk of dialogue. At certain points in our questions back and forth, we each could discern the presence of a reconciling spirit. The story of that encounter can be found on pages 169-171 of this book.

Saudis and Americans have a long journey still ahead in order to find unity. Divisive issues exist to be sure. Saudis have an important dialogue that is needed with other Muslims in different countries. Whatever outward differences remain, the necessity and reward of dialogue and cultural exchange is paramount. As urged by an early Quaker minister, Isaac Penington,

> . . . it is not the different practice from one another that breaks the peace and unity [of God], but the judging of one another because of different practices…For this is the true ground of love and unity, not that such a man walks and does just as I do, but because I feel the same Spirit and Life in him, and that he walks in his rank, in his own order, in his proper way and place of subjection to that; and this is far more pleasing to me than if he walked just in that track wherein I walk.

As a step toward trusting our abilities to resolve those differences in time, Dr. Alhomoudi's depth of knowledge about Qur'anic and Prophetic Tradition, his close observation of culture, and his own desire to help foster a peaceful global society make this journal a contribution to a challenging and necessary dialogue between two different cultures, American and Saudi.

The daily entries in this three-month journal cover a wide variety of themes.

The chapter titles name predominant ones but within each chapter readers will find engaging anecdotes that mirror to us Americans what we look like and will help Saudis to know us. Again, Dr. Alhomoudi invites readers to contact him about any errors or misconceptions. In Chapter One, we meet each of the other Fulbright scholars who will reappear throughout the story. In Chapter Two, Dr. Alhomoudi presents the particular tools for dialogue learned during the orientation weeks. Chapters Three and Four describe his in-depth study of Christianity, needed in order to place in correct context the Baptists, Quakers, Lutherans, Amish, and Catholics he was meeting. Chapter Five investigates even further the historical background necessary for effective dialogue. The State Department gathered all the Fulbright activists together in Denver half-way through their sojourn in order to meet Native Americans and study with them their history and spirituality; Chapter Six records that extraordinary weekend. Chapter Seven explores culture and pop culture from early Christianity to Hip-Hop. Then, finally in Chapter Eight, Dr. Alhomoudi describes farewells, and elucidates insights learned and actions taken as a result of his journeys in prayer and travel.

These themes need further discussion rooted in critical thinking and dialogue to help interpret how people of devout faith can remain faithful to tradition as well as accommodate inevitable change. The friendships formed as a result of the Fulbright 2008 encounters in America are still strong and growing. Each in his or her own country is striving to increase understanding among persons who claim important religious and cultural differences; each is seeking justice and peace. As we go forward, we will need much patience and courage. These interfaith activist scholars in their striving for a peaceful and just coexistence among religious traditions are the community to which I feel a deep sense of belonging. I think each of them would join me in these hopeful words from the American Quaker minister John Woolman (1746),

> *Our gracious Creator cares and provides for all his creatures. His tender mercies are over all his works and so far as true love influences our minds, so far as we become interested in [God's] workmanship and feel a desire to make use of every opportunity to lessen the distresses of the afflicted and to increase the happiness of the creation.*

17

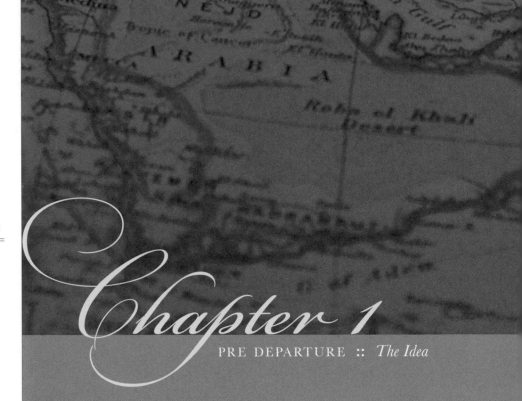

Chapter 1

PRE DEPARTURE :: *The Idea*

"Write to be understood."

Lawrence Clark Powell, American Librarian, (1906-2001)

} In early June of 2008, the Consultant of the Rector of Imam Muhammad bin Saud Islamic University in Riyadh asked me to nominate professors for the U.S. Fulbright Interfaith Action Program (ICAP). I was able to come up with only a few names. As a result, he asked me whether I could participate in this program. I firmly rejected the idea as this was not our first discussion about it. Then he asked me a very simple question: "Why not?" I had no easy answer for him so I requested a few days to find a suitable answer.

As I reflected, I visualized the ugly political picture of the United States of America, with its wars against Muslim terrorists and its hegemonic attitude toward Muslim countries. I wondered, "What do Americans want with this dialogue among the faiths?" I was skeptical. Should I be involved with the arrogance and potential manipulative agenda of American political policy and behavior? But I stopped this way of thinking. I reminded myself that I actually know many Americans and consider many of them my friends. None of them is either arrogant or participates in any manipulative agenda. So where did this idea, this prejudice come from? I mulled over these possible misconceptions and began to consider serious participation in the ICAP program. I needed only to take one last important step of discernment.

Even as an adult, before any of my major decisions are final, I consult my parents out of respect for their wisdom. We share lunch on a regular basis and during that time, my siblings and I discuss personal or family matters with our parents. I proposed the idea of the Fulbright Program and my dad surprised me when he told me, "Son, if they want to have a dialogue, it is okay to participate." I asked my mom what she thought. They work as a team, and if there are reservations, she will help them be discussed. My parents consider the pros and cons of a choice and their views while I listen. Afterwards, I am trusted to choose wisely. In this case, they had no further conversation and it was clear they both supported the choice should I decide to go to the U.S. as a Fulbright Scholar.

One has to be careful when moving from ideas to words and then from words into action. I continued to think it over. I also consulted a few friends with different views. My Atheist friend was very frank when he plainly asked me if my reason for participating in this three-month program was to escape from hypocritical multi-faced social situations in Saudi Arabia where everyone must wear two or more social masks. My clear and unequivocal answer was NO! Then he suggested that I participate and have fun. His attitude comes from his philosophy that dialogue among faiths is just like flipping the same coin. In other words, for him the religions tell the same story with different storytellers. Although I expected such an answer from him, I felt that asking him was a must. Others had totally different opinions, from those who thought it would be a waste of time and effort to those who believe that these programs were designed to serve certain agendas, with no explanation of what these agendas are, or to whom they belong. Others refused the whole idea altogether and didn't care to discuss it with me. None of the arguments against interfaith dialogue of civilizations convinced me to withhold my participation. So with a clear conscience and support from my family, I decided to apply.

As a participant, I wanted to help dispel ignorance and to build cooperative relationships in our troubled times. I also saw the opportunity to create a substantial basis for community social action. In my statement of purpose for the application, I concluded that my special interest was to develop interfaith dialogue within the Kingdom of Saudi Arabia. On July 30, 2008, I received my nomination for the Fulbright ICAP program and began my plans to travel to the U.S. in September.

. .. .

DAY ONE :: SATURDAY
SEPTEMBER 13, 2008
"Sometimes I'm confused by what I think is really obvious. But what I think is really obvious obviously isn't obvious..."

— Michael Stipe, American Singer, (1960-)

I arrived in Philadelphia, Pennsylvania, weary after hours of travel from my home in Riyadh, Saudi Arabia. I felt hesitant, anxious, enthusiastic, excited, challenged, and curious.

. .. .

DAY TWO :: SUNDAY
SEPTEMBER 14, 2008
"Curiosity is one of the great secrets of happiness."

— Bryant H. McGill, American Poet, (1969-)

On this day I met the people who would become my community for the next three months. Their backgrounds predicted rich learning and good friendships for our group.

Dr. Ziad Elias Fahd is an Assistant Professor in the Department of Social and Behavioral Sciences as well as an Assistant Director of Student Affairs at Notre Dame University in Beirut, Lebanon. Dr. Fahd received an M.A. and Ph.D. in Theology from the Catholic University of Lyon in France. His interests include Religion and Public Debate, Social Issues, and Pluralism. He contributes to the Arab Theological Encyclopedia, along with writing "The Non-Violent Approach to the Crisis of the Middle East." Dr. Fahd also hosts a weekly television program on the impact of Christian faith on Lebanese religious pluralism.

Mousse Khedimellah is a Muslim scholar from Paris, France. He has joined the Boniuk Center for Religious Tolerance at Rice University. Mr. Khedimellah is a Manager in Sustainable Development in a large multinational French company. He is the co-founder of the Muslim Brotherhood against Anti-Semitism and Islamophobia (MBA). He holds an M.A. in Sociology of Religion, with a focus on Islam, from the School for Advanced Studies in the Social Sciences (EHESS) in France. He researches issues related to interfaith dialogue in diverse cultural and societal settings. He is very interested in the confluence between religion and business and religion and sustainability.

Serge Hyacinthe Mousse Triode from Burkina Faso, Africa, is a Catholic missionary priest for the Society of the Missionaries of Africa. He received an M.A. in Interreligious Studies, specializing in Islam from the Institute of Studies of Religions and Culture (Pontifical Gregorian University), a Diploma in Islamic Studies from the Pontifical Institute of Arabic and Islamic Studies, and a Baccalaureate in Sacred Theology from the Catholic University of Eastern Africa. His interests include Dialogue among religions particularly between Muslims and Christians, including such dialogue amidst the recovery from conflict in Rwanda. Traore's published works include "Encounters in Rwanda," and articles for different Christian magazines like *Voix D'Afrique* and *Petit Echo*.

. . ..

DAY THREE :: MONDAY
SEPTEMBER 15, 2008
"An intellectual is a man who takes more words than necessary to tell more than he knows."
— Dwight Eisenhower, 34th American President, (1890-1969)

Today, more introductions.

Fr. Michael Chua Kim Wah of Malaysia serves as Parish Priest of the Church of the Visitation for the Roman Catholic Archdiocese of Kuala Lumpur and Ecclesiastical Assistant of Archdiocesan Ministry of Ecumenical and Interreligious Affairs. Fr. Michael has a degree in law (LLB) from the University of Malaya and a BA degree in Theology from College General Regional Major Seminary in Malaysia. He is actively involved in promoting interreligious/ intercultural dialogue at grassroots and involved in interreligious and civil rights activism at both national and regional levels. He has also published works, given lectures and organized workshops, seminars, conferences on Interreligious Dialogue, Ecumenism, Intercultural Dialogue,

Race/ Ethnic Relations among Muslims, Buddhists, Hindus, Taoist, Sikhs and Christians.

Next is Ms. Mehri Niknam, the Iranian Jewish woman who now lives in England where she is the Executive Director and Founder of the Joseph Interfaith Foundation, the only officially registered joint Muslim-Jewish NGO in England. She describes herself as an Islamophile Jew. She has been a consultant in Muslim-Jewish Relations for over 15 years. Ms Niknam received both BA and MA degrees in Jewish and Hebrew Studies from Leo Baeck College, London, specializing in Judaism and Islam in the Medieval Period. She has also studied classical Persian literature and has lectured extensively on all subjects at various universities, including the University of London. She has also initiated conferences at the University of London on these topics. Ms Niknam received the prestigious MBE award in 2005 from the Her Majesty Queen Elizabeth II of England for her contributions to Muslim-Jewish Relations in Britain, and is a member of two governmental roundtable interfaith think tanks in the UK.

Dr. Fatimah Hussein, a Muslim sister from Indonesia, serves as Executive Director of Indonesian Consortium of Religious Studies, a consortium of three universities: Gadjah Mada University, State Islamic University, and Duta Wacana Christian University in Yogyakarta, Indonesia. She teaches in a multiple appointment on the faculties of State Islamic University, Gadjah Mada University, and Indonesian Islamic University, teaching Interreligious Dialogue, Islamic Philosophy, and Islamic Thought and Civilization. She served on the steering committee for various international conferences. She received her M.A. in Islamic Philosophy at McGill University, Canada, and a Ph.D. in Asian Studies at Melbourne University, Australia. Her published doctorate is "Muslim-Christian Relations in Indonesia: The Exclusivist and Inclusivity Muslims' Perspectives." She writes, lectures, facilitates, consults, and actively serves on committees in Indonesia and the region.

Dr. Akhtarul Shaukat Ali Hairat Wasey heads the Department of Islamic Studies in the Zakir Husain Institute of Islamic Studies at Jamia Milia Islamia University. Professor Wasey received an M.A. in Islamic Studies and Theology from Aligarh Muslim University. He has supervised 17 Ph.D. research scholars, and has written 25 works including "Islamic Responses to Contemporary Challenges," and "Education of Indian Muslims." Wasey is active in the UN, most recently being appointed General Secretary of the South Asia Inter-Religious Council on HIV/AIDS.

Mr. Ghassan Abdel Salaam Manasra of Israel is the Imam and Sheik of the Qadri Sufi Center, Director of the Anwar Il-Salaam NGO, and Teacher of Sufi Philosophy and Islamic Studies. Mr. Manasra is working on an M.A. in Arabic Literature and Language at Hebrew University, and has completed two B.A.'s in Islamic and Middle Eastern Studies from the same institution. His interests include Muslim-Christian Dialogue, Sufism, and Conflict Resolution. Mr. Manasra has published and led conferences on these topic and leads tours of mosques, churches and synagogues for leaders of other faiths.

We met one another under the auspices of the Dialogue Institute and its staff at Temple University. Their job was to help us get acquainted and orient us to our three-month stay in the U.S., each of us would continue to a different institution of higher education after our first weeks of orientation in Philadelphia.

One of our first interactive exercises included sharing life stories that were either very sad or very happy. At my turn, I remembered a book I read a long time ago by Sayyed Qutb in which he described Americans as naïve people who believe anything they hear. He wrote about meeting some at his university and telling them that people in Egypt eat watermelon with salt and pepper. His American friends tried doing so and said they liked it. Qutb made fun of them for believing him. I thought I would try my own experiment; I would tell the group a story that was not really so sad to see how they might react. My story was about a cat that we had back home who was ten days old when another cat had a fight with her and injured her. As I expected, some said, "Oh, how sad! I could read in their eyes, however, that they knew I was not serious. This story proves to me that the myth spread out about Americans that they are naïve is nothing but a myth. I believe the Americans with Qutb were just being kind, but what Qutb was doing, or trying to do, was wrong as he should not lie just to make fun of them. Tough American leaders and fellows, like Hillary Clinton, would dare to precisely state that "The American people are tired of liars and people who pretend to be something they're not."

. . ..

DAY FOUR :: TUESDAY
SEPTEMBER 16, 2008
"When we make college more affordable, we make the American dream more achievable."
— William J. Clinton, 42nd American President, (1946-)

As we continued to introduce ourselves and get to know one another, we discussed academic background and interest. In our discussion, I shared with the group two of my recently published articles; "Islamic Law and the Modern State: Conflict or Co-Existence," and "World Muslim Council." I hoped to spark discussion, but these opening sessions went in a different direction.

The first session was a meditation session — a first for me. Our facilitator asked us to take our places around the room and sit relaxed with our eyes closed. She then directed us in a quiet voice to think back to our childhood and the first home we lived in and to a spot in our home where we had felt most comfortable. She expanded further by asking us to remember the first community we grew up in and then recall our first place of worship and how we began to know God. She called us from the past to the present, asking us to ponder where we are now and what our hopes for the world are. I was not sure of the point of this

23

meditation, but I enjoyed it and thought that people who were tired could nap.

The second session was equally confusing when another facilitator asked us to name our heroes or someone whom we admire. Everyone mentioned a person of merit in his or her life: a father, a grandfather, the sheik *tariqa* (leader of a mystical path), Martin Luther King, or a school supervisor. This time I stopped the process to ask what was the point of raising questions about our "hero." The hero, I came to understand, has traits for each of us that could well be ones that help us realize our hopes for the world. That understanding helped. I also wanted to understand the point of the meditation as these approaches to study were so different than I had expected. Again, I learned that meditation is a practical kind of worship among several religions, including Christianity. It helps relax the mind in order to aid reflection and study. Akhtarul Wasey spoke about a Sufi understanding in Islam called "*mukashafah*" and "*muhasabah*," two Arabic words that mean self-observing and self-revising. I know the Arabic meaning of those two words, but I did not recognize them as mystical practices. In Saudi Arabia, Sufism, and mysticism in general, are not openly practiced. Perhaps we are missing an important part of Islam in Saudi Arabia. Although I have tried many things in my life, I have never experienced Sufism, so I decided to add it to my "experience to-do list."

In our third session with a professor from the College of Education at Temple University, the professor spoke at length about his family and how Jews were rejected in the 1950s. He has dedicated his life to theories and practices of education that do not alienate and isolate people. He trains teachers and administrators in democratic ethical educational leadership. I began to consider how education shapes intercultural and interreligious dialogue.

First, I recognized once again how educators connect personal story and theory. But to better understand the relationship of education to cultural and religious formation, I learned what I could of the basic American educational system in contrast to ours in Saudi Arabia.

Compulsory education has been a part of America since its Colonial stage. American education is composed of three required stages, and several other optional stages. All children are required to attend elementary school, where they are taught basic Language Arts, Mathematics, and Science. Elementary classes are usually eight hours long, with long breaks for lunch and physical activity. Unlike the schooling system in Saudi Arabia where we have specialized teachers for each subject, in America one teacher gives lessons on all subjects to these young children. Elementary school begins with kindergarten, which begins when the child is five, and continues for five or six more grade levels. Each grade level is nine months long, with summers off. Students attend middle school for fifth or sixth through eighth grade. High school is a four-grade program beginning with ninth grade. The school day is broken into seven or eight equal blocks that are each dedicated to a given subject, usually about 45 minutes, plus a lunch break. Each grade has several

required courses, but also has some elective choices; students can take special classes
to pursue an interest or develop a skill. Traditional electives are foreign languages, Art,
Metalwork, or Life Sciences, like Psychology. High school students are 14 to 18 years
old. Elementary, middle, and high school are required by law and are provided by state
governments. Although there are public schools, private schools are also available and
state approved. In Saudi Arabia the two years before elementary school, preschool and
kindergarten are usually attended in private schools. Elementary schools are six years
long, followed by three years of secondary school, then three years of high school. These
differences are small however, in contrast with our cultural differences about gender. In
Saudi, boys and girls are taught in separate schools through adulthood; in the U.S. few
schools practice this segregation though certain private religious schools do.

After high school, most American students pursue a Bachelor of Art or Bachelor of
Science degree. The first American college was Harvard University, founded in 1636. It
continues to set the standard for college and university entrance which is on a competitive
basis. Public American colleges and universities can either be state-funded or privately-
funded. Many private schools have religious funding; for example, the University of
Notre Dame is funded by the Catholic Church's Dominican Order. Most Bachelor
programs last four years, and are focused on a specific Science or discipline, like Biology
or Philosophy.

I noted what I thought could be one reason Americans in general are comfortable
with religious pluralism. At the elementary, secondary, high school, and university levels,
religion is taught as an academic subject but not as a belief system to be practiced. Thus
students learn morality indirectly but not necessarily theology and disciplines of practice
as is the case in Saudi Arabia. Thus by young adulthood, Americans are aware of
different religions as options and they may not yet have chosen a particular religious path.

At the university level, students can begin working on research through an internship.
Students seeking a Bachelor of Science degree will often be required to work as an aid
in a laboratory or experimental setting. Those seeking a Bachelor of Arts may teach or
apprentice in a studio. They can then pursue Masters degrees, two-year programs that
allow for a specific focus in a field, and Doctoral degrees, which qualify one to teach and
do research in a university. Scientific research in the United States occurs either through
government programs or private programs, which can be associated with a university or
with a business. University research is funded by grants from foundations interested in
a certain problem or field; scientists must present their experiment to the foundation in
order to receive the money to carry it out. There are people whose sole occupations are
writing proposals to acquire grants. Universities publish research in order to contribute
to the development of the field. Companies fund research through their profits, and
keep their research private so that they can produce a marketable product from it. Large
companies, like in the pharmaceutical industry, can devote profits to discovering drugs,

and then patent the technology to ensure that no one copies their results for profit. Finding the balance between research for profit and for cure can be difficult; striving to link research and public good is a model worth trying.

This trend of linking higher education to research at the university level has been adopted in Saudi Arabia only recently. The increase in making this link is commensurate with a tremendous change in the number of institutions in recent years. The Ministry of Higher Education in Saudi Arabia used to administer only seven universities which were run by the government; now there are over twenty governmental universities and over ten private universities. Still, however, Saudi Arabia does not have community colleges. The specialized research university is also a new trend with King Abdullah of Saudi Arabia's establishment of the King Abdullah University for Science and Technology (KAUST) whose budget exceeds the combined total of all other Saudi universities.

In our last session today Dr. Leonard Swidler presented a PowerPoint overview of the seven stages of deep dialogue. In his experience, persons who choose to grow through meeting and engaging with others who live different faith traditions will encounter these stages. The first stage is the radical encounter of differences in which one may or may not actually participate with the other. The second stage is crossing over, in other words, letting go and entering the world of others, ready to get to know and understand them and them you. Then the third stage is living in or experiencing the world of others; this leads to the fourth stage which is crossing back into one's own culture or faith tradition with expanded vision. This exchange should lead to the fifth stage which is the dialogic awakening; this pivotal stage includes a radical paradigm shift in which the ability to respect one's own tradition can happen at the same time one respects a different tradition as well. Consequently, a global awakening occurs in the sixth stage when the paradigm shift matures. The seventh stage and the fruit of the dialogue is the personal and global transforming of life and behavior to create peace and sustainability. Well, as sweet as they look, these seven stages might not happen in such a precise order or happen with ease. People grow and change in different times and ways which deserve consideration. But I understood the basic movement and was aware that I, myself, was experiencing this movement among the stages of my journey.

. . ..

DAY FIVE :: WEDNESDAY
SEPTEMBER 17, 2008

"If the freedom of speech is taken away then dumb and silent we may be led, like sheep to the slaughter."

— George Washington, 1st American President, (1732-1799)

Today, one of our tours was to see the murals painted on whole building walls throughout the city of Philadelphia. By coincidence, I was reading Al-Riyadh newspaper, a locally popular newspaper in Saudi Arabia, and on that day its public opinion poll was about writing and drawing on the walls of the city of Riyadh. Approximately sixty percent of the Saudi readers were not in favor of writing on walls and considered it to be an uncivilized behavior. Philadelphia galvanized its youth to stop creating graffiti and paint art instead — a courageous and creative initiative. Other cities are beginning to adopt this Philadelphian phenomenon. In the Al-Riyadh poll, I voted to increase the paintings and artificial drawing on the street walls.

The rest of our day focused on the founding of America and its form of government. We started at the Constitution Center. The Constitution of the United States outlines the overall system and powers of the United States federal government and powers of the states. It was unanimously approved on September 17, 1787 and is the basis for all American law.

The constitution's unique quality is its flexibility; the Constitution can be changed in two ways. First, two-thirds of both the House and the Senate can propose a Constitutional Amendment. Second, two-thirds of the states can hold a convention in which they propose an Amendment. No states have made this latter choice. When three-fourths of all state legislatures approve an Amendment, it is simply appended to the Constitution and becomes law. This process can be long and arduous. For example, the most recent 27th Amendment was finally ratified in 1992, but was originally put before the states in 1789. The 27th Amendment prohibits any law that increases or decreases the salary of members of the Congress from taking effect, until the start of the next set of terms of office for Representatives. It is the most recent amendment to the United States Constitution, having been ratified in 1992, more than 202 years after its initial submission in 1789.

The Bill of Rights is an addition to the Constitution that specifies a series of rights guaranteed to all American citizens. It is made up of the first ten Amendments to the Constitution, and was included to satisfy concerns about the perceived excessive power of a centralized federal government. Of these, the 1st Amendment is the most famous and most controversial.

The 1st Amendment ensures that Americans have the right to worship freely, to speak and to write freely, and to gather in peaceful assembly. The 1st Amendment is often employed in court cases about obscenity, sedition, and protest, with varying results. The Supreme Court governs the interpretation of what "free speech" is, and generally prohibits speech that causes danger or harm, like shouting "Fire!" to cause a panic or spreading lies for slanderous purposes, or obscenity, like words that cannot be said on television — although pornography is generally legal. The Court is clear that opinions can be freely aired; in 1977, the American Civil Liberties Union (ACLU), a non-profit group of lawyers and activists dedicated to civil rights, reversed laws in Skokie, Illinois, a largely Jewish suburb of Chicago, prohibiting Neo-Nazi parades and demonstrations.

The 1st Amendment is also important in the separation of church and state. The Amendment prohibits both the restriction of religious worship and the government supporting any one religion. Public Christmas or Ten Commandment displays on state property and prayer in schools have been removed, but the Court has ruled that money can be given to secular institutions run by religious groups, like Catholic hospitals. This practice has become more relevant with President Bush's and President Obama's commitment to the government funding of "faith-based initiatives," religious groups that perform social services. The Court has also regulated how religion can be expressed: while the law can regulate practices, it cannot regulate beliefs, and can only regulate practices where the State has a "compelling interest" in the practice and if the practice can be regulated without reference to a particular group. Hence polygamy, which Mormons used to practice, is illegal, but ritual animal sacrifice is permitted, as in the 1993 case of the Church of the Lukumi Babalu Aye, which slaughtered and ate animals as a part of its worship. The Court overturned the law passed by the local city that tried to prohibit their worship under new animal cruelty laws.

Finally, the American press enjoys almost total freedom to print anything except outright lies. Only a few restrictions have been imposed: newspapers cannot print articles that would result in "substantial evils" or "lawless actions," restrictions arising specifically from World War I, where tracts were being distributed to convince people not to respond to the draft; and schools can restrict what is written in school papers. Libel is much more difficult to prosecute in the United States than, in Europe for example, because the Court has ruled that printed words are only libel if the plaintiff can prove "actual malice." State laws vary, however, and certain states hold that some categories of statements are of themselves defamatory, so that malice does not need to be proved, for example, calling someone a leper.

Next we visited Independence Hall, constructed between 1732 and 1753. It was a symbol of the nation to come. Independence Hall is, by every estimate, the birthplace of the United States. It was within its walls that the Declaration of Independence was deliberated and adopted. It was there that the Constitution of the United States was debated, drafted and signed. That document is the oldest federal constitution in existence and was framed by a convention of delegates from 12 of the original 13 colonies. Notable among the document's many innovative features is the separation of powers among the Legislative (Congress), Executive (President), and Judicial branches of government. Also important is that the Congress was split into two houses. The Senate gives equal power to all the states regardless of size. The House of Representatives gives proportional representation according to size. Bicameral Congress consists of the Senate (100 seats, 2 members are elected from each state by popular vote to serve six-year terms; one-third are elected every two years) and the House of Representatives (435 seats; members are directly elected by popular vote to serve two-year terms). The Judicial system consists of the Supreme Court (nine justices; nominated by the President and confirmed with the advice and consent of the Senate; appointed to serve for life); the United States Courts of Appeal; United States District Courts; State and County Courts.

Then we stopped at the Liberty Bell. The Pennsylvania Assembly ordered the Bell forged in 1751 to commemorate the 50-year anniversary of William Penn's 1701 Charter of Privileges, Pennsylvania's original Constitution. This document speaks of the rights and freedoms valued by people the world over. Particularly forward-thinking were Penn's ideas on religious freedom, his liberal stance on Native American rights, and his inclusion of citizens in enacting laws. The Liberty Bell gained iconic importance when abolitionists adopted it as a symbol in their efforts to put an end to slavery throughout America. The final expansion of a crack happened on Washington's Birthday in 1846 and the Bell could no longer ring. Tradition says that a spider built a web in this crack to protect the bell. This story reminded me of the spider story in Islam when a spider built a web on the cave where Prophet Muhammad, peace be upon him, was hiding from Quraish, his tribe, in order to protect him.

29

DAY SIX: THURSDAY
SEPTEMBER 18, 2008
"We must learn to live together as brothers or perish together as fools."
— Martin Luther King Jr., American Activist, (1929-1968)

D r. Reuven Firestone began our study of Muslim and Jewish relations with, a personal story that has led to two of his books: *Teaching Judaism to Muslims* and *Teaching Islam to Jews.* He grew up in an upper-middle class family, and at a young age went to Israel expecting to meet intelligent Jews and an ignorant, violent Arab community. What he found was different; he instead found plenty of violence among his Jewish community. Even after rabbinical studies and a Ph.D., Firestone contends that education and friendship, not theology, afford the best way to understand each other.

His own experience on sabbatical in Egypt with his family provides an example. Many of his Jewish friends warned him not to endanger his kids, but he went anyway. The Egyptian school welcomed his children as the first Jewish students at the school, but advised the children not to tell other students that they were Jewish until they had made friendships in the school community. They also advised that the family not engage in any discussion related to the Arab-Israeli conflict, that they should listen only and not talk. Firestone agreed and was surprised by what he heard. The Egyptians he heard saw the Americans as more violent than the Arabs. Firestone understood how prejudice works when he realized that the Americans see the Arabs the same way, wondering how mothers and fathers could send their children to kill others and feel happy to see bloody wars based on winning and losing. What he learned confirmed for him the importance of real friendships despite differences.

One of the most important ways to build those friendships and to engage issues in the dialogue among civilizations is to learn the language of the person you don't know and may fear; no one can understand Judaism without understanding the language for example. So Firestone learned Arabic and felt capable to teach Islam to Jews, obviously not to Muslims. It is the same for Muslims; they cannot learn and know Judaism without learning Hebrew. This piece of education is the most important.

At the end of this engaging session, I raised a question about this need to know the language of "the other." I wondered whether it would be so necessary for Muslims to learn Hebrew if they simply accepted what Prophet Muhammad, peace be upon him, taught about Jews.

Firestone insisted that the learning of the language was essential to dispel the inherent distrust between Jews and Muslims. In general, he felt that Jews believe that Muslims are two-faced, that they will say something in the dialogue and say something else among themselves; he adds that he expects that Muslims must think the same about Jews.

I commented that such a strong distrust means basically that there is no hope for dialogue. Firestone answered that his comment was a generalization and not necessarily the case for all Jews and Muslims. Those who can dialogue must.

There were several questions at the end of the session, and I raised two questions, one leading to the other. The first question was "Why do we find Islamic studies department in many western universities, but there are no departments for Judaic or Christian Studies in Islamic universities?" Before Firestone answered the question, several colleagues mentioned that there are some departments in Islamic universities, for example Professor Wasey said there is one at Delhi at the Jamiaa Milla Islamia, another at the University of Dacca in Bangladesh, and Ein Shams University has a similar department. Firestone then said he had no answer for this question, and would like to hear my answer. My answer was embedded in the second question. I returned to the point in his lecture where he said that to learn about another religion one must learn their language. For Jews and Christians who want to learn about Islam while studying Arabic makes sense as the religion is new to them. To learn the Arabic language is the only way to be able to understand the Quran. On the other hand, if Muslims believe in Prophet Muhammad, then they only need to learn about his teachings about Jews and Christians, and to learn what the Quran says about them. There is no need to learn Hebrew. Prophet Muhammad explained in great detail how to deal with a Jewish neighbor or with a Jewish trader as well as how to treat Christians. He also taught how to deal with Jewish and Christian religious texts, both scriptural and oral. Therefore, Muslims do not need to study Judaism, Christianity, or Hebrew because Prophet Muhammad has already clarified the relationships. Would Professor Firestone agree with me or not?

Firestone insisted on his position that Muslims still need to learn Hebrew to learn about Judaism and Christianity because for him the texts revealed by Prophet Muhammad were contradictory. For example, in some prophetic traditions the Prophet directs his companions to follow the Jews while in some other prophetic traditions he directs them to oppose what the Jews do. To learn each other's languages allows for each person to interpret for him or herself, he thought.

I found his premise deficient as I see no contradiction in the Prophet's teaching. During the years when Prophet Muhammad was in Mecca and during his early years in Medina, he considered the Jew's tradition as divine, so he would follow them as long as there was no alternative Islamic teaching. Once he received any alternative revelation, he would instruct his companions to follow the new revelation instead of the Jew's tradition because he considered the Islamic revelation as the last and most complete version of God's revelation. With respect for the dialogue, we agreed to disagree.

In the rest of the day we began to see why such dialogue is so important. At the office of the Chaplain at the University of Pennsylvania, we heard the story of one student from a Jewish Orthodox background explain how a Muslim-Jewish experience influenced

her. She and 25 other students, all either Jewish or Muslim, went for ten days to help rebuild destroyed homes and relationships with the people in mosques and synagogues in Louisiana after hurricane Katrina had ravaged the area. They chose this work over a beach vacation during their school break. Upon their return to campus, the UPenn newspaper ran an article entitled, "Jewish students going for jihad," in which Muslim students were accused of involving the Jews in their activities to prepare them for jihad. The article showed very little understanding of jihad and displayed instead the very prejudices the Muslim and Jewish students were trying to undo. At least they had done so for themselves, a good step.

The students' dialogue covers a wide range of topics. Sometimes they discuss complicated religious issues, and sometimes more surface ones. Simple questions like "Why do Muslim women wear Hijab?" can lead to new understandings. One student, who was an Orthodox Jew, found that her Muslim peers were able to understand her better than some of her Jewish-American friends when it comes to questions related to having a friendship or relationship with a member of the opposite sex.

Interfaith projects as "Walk the Walk" at the Interfaith Center at the Episcopal Cathedral are paving the way for this progress we observed at the college level. In this program high school students from a neighborhood mosque, church, and synagogue agree to study and work together for nine months. They study sacred texts and do service projects together, then reflect on their experiences and how their views of the differing faith traditions are growing and maturing. If enough young people can receive this quality of religious education, then perhaps religious violence can stop.

Our last visit of the day was to the Mishkan Shalom Synagogue where we adults could practice more good dialogue. We arrived three minutes before sunset when those Muslims who were fasting were due to break their fast. Our hosts respectfully changed the program and started with dinner. The rabbi recited a heartfelt poem as a prayer that set the tone for our visit.

I notice that no one touched the Torah even when they read it,
they use a small stick with a head like a hand, and they call
it "yad," which means in Hebrew and Arabic "hand."

A prayer for the journey
We could say it everyday
When we first leave the soft warmth of our beds
And do not know for sure if we will return at night
When we get in the trains, planes and automobiles
And put our lives in the hands of many strangers
Or when we leave our homes for a day, a week, a month or more-
Will we return to a peaceful home? Untouched by fire, flood, or crime?
How will our travel change us?
What gives us the courage to go through that door?

A prayer for the journey
For the journey we take in this fragile vessel of flesh
A finite number of years and we will reach
The unknown, where it all began
Every life, every day, every hour is a journey
In the travel is the discovery,
The wisdom, the joy
Every life, every day, every hour is a journey
In the travel is the reward,
The peace, the pleasing

The food, prepared by a member of the synagogue, was extremely delicious and was not very different from the Arabian cuisine I knew. After the dinner we had an opportunity to go upstairs where the prayers are held. Interestingly, this synagogue is one of few synagogues in the city of Philadelphia, the rest of the synagogues are in the suburbs. I noticed in several places that Jews move on to establish new neighborhoods that include new synagogues, schools, and Jewish social centers, and when they move they sell their homes, synagogues, centers for a profit. Then they re-establish themselves in new neighborhood.

During and after dinner I had a long interesting conversation with David, a rabbinical student in his second academic year. We discussed the Judaic Law and ventured to see if there is similarity in legal theories between the Judaic and Islamic Law. Indeed, there is a great similarity, but David preferred to put me in contact with one of his professors to get more accurate answers. Then, Michael, another rabbinical student, joined us shortly and a couple of days later Michael linked me with Rabbi David with whom I still exchange emails. David, the rabbinical student, went with me and the group upstairs where they preserve the Torah and read it. I noticed that no one touched the Torah even when they read it; instead, they use a small stick with a head like a hand, and they call it "*yad*," which means in Hebrew and Arabic "hand." After looking at and reading from the Torah, we were introduced to the "*shovar*" that is a horn which Jews blow in their New Year, "*roshashanah*" which means to gather. I tried it out, and found how difficult it is to blow the *shovar*.

. . . .

DAY SEVEN :: FRIDAY
SEPTEMBER 19, 2008

"Twenty years from now you will be more disappointed by the things that you didn't do than by the ones you did do. So throw off the bowlines. Sail away from the safe harbor. Catch the trade winds in your sails. Explore. Dream. Discover."

— Mark Twain, American Writer, (1835-1910)

Our first week closed with a Shabbat celebration at sundown as is the Jewish practice. One of our seminar leaders, Dr. Racelle Weiman joined one of our participants, Ms. Mehri Niknam, in leading a Sabbath celebration. The sharing of a meal and of stories of reconciliation helped us see how the practice of Sabbath is about peacemaking in addition to a time for rest. The Sabbath celebrates God's creation of Heaven and Earth in six days and then God's invitation to rest on the seventh day, the Sabbath. I think the practice of celebrating the Sabbath is one of the biggest differences between Islam and Judaism. Muslims believe that God created all of creation in seven days but that He needed no rest or sleep. I would learn more about this Jewish ritual as our weeks progressed.

. . . .

DAY EIGHT :: SATURDAY
SEPTEMBER 20, 2008

"Eskimo: If I did not know about God and sin, would I go to Hell? Priest: No, not if you did not know. Eskimo: Then why did you tell me?"

— Annie Dillard, American Author, (1945-)

This was our first free day. Because several of us were becoming friends in just this first full week, we decided to spend the day together discovering Philadelphia. The time gave me a chance to continue the sincere Christian-Muslim dialogue I had started with Serge. Our Catholic from Lebanon is the humorist in the group, but avoided discussing his own religious background. Serge didn't seem to mind, so I put some of my questions to him. I and other non-Christians have wondered about the apparent plurality reflected in the Christian Bible, especially in the four differing gospel accounts of Jesus' life. Why the differences? I asked Serge.

While Christians believe that the authors of the scriptural accounts were inspired by God, they do not believe that these authors were simply recording the words that Jesus dictated or that they were mysteriously entranced while writing. They remained very human. Just like other historians, these authors selected data from the numerous events associated with Jesus' life and compiled it into a synthetic whole in order to communicate a point. Because there were four authors, each of whom was historically situated, there are today four nuanced accounts of Jesus' life. The minor differences in their accounts do not compromise their truthfulness. Instead, the differences make the accounts more vivid.

Like the companions of the Prophet Mohammad retelling varying accounts of his life, Christians read the four presentations of Jesus' life in this way. By reading the four accounts together, while being careful not to minimize each distinct message, Christians are presented with a complete picture of who Jesus was.

I also learned from him, that in order to understand Christianity one must absorb the structure and the concept of the church. According to the Christian Scriptures, Jesus ascended into Heaven after his resurrection. Just before this event he gave his disciples one last command: "Go into the world and make disciples, baptizing them in the name of the Father, Son, and Holy Spirit, and teaching them what I have taught you."

The New Testament book of Acts tells the story of the earliest disciples' attempt to follow Jesus' last command. In it the disciple Luke records how the small sect that claimed to have met the risen Jesus eventually became a Mediterranean phenomenon, with followers spread out from Jerusalem to Rome. This group continued to grow, and today those people who adhere to the teachings of Jesus call themselves "the church." What do Christians believe about the church?

First, they believe that the church is the place where those who want to learn how to follow Jesus today can find sympathetic people who will aid them in their journey. The church has been called "the family of God," because it is a place where love and sympathy are supposed to reign supreme.

Second, Christians believe that the church is the place where, Jesus continues to have a mysterious presence in the world. This is why the church was called "the body of Christ" in the New Testament. As Christ ascended into Heaven, he promised his disciples that he would send an "encourager," the Holy Spirit, whose presence in their hearts would be the very presence of Christ. Jesus also told his disciples, "Where two or more of you gather together in my name, I am there with you."

Third, they believe that the church is the instrument God uses to continue to foster the worldwide peace that was initiated in Jesus' life, death, and resurrection. Jesus referred to the church as a "city on a hill," because it is a refuge for the hopeless; and it is "the salt of the Earth," because it both preserves and seasons humanity with God's love.

Fourth, they believe that the church is not bound to a specific place but that it occurs wherever believers gather together to worship God. Christian worship has always been a corporate affair. Although the spirituality of the individual drives the authenticity of Christianity, it is the Christian community that gives the individual his or her identity. Walls of a building do not make a Christian, but Christianity has always been a religion of community. This last explanation answered one of the more frequently asked questions among non-Christians I have met.

How wonderful for me from Saudi Arabia to have this first real interfaith encounter with Serge, who is from Rwanda, and to discuss what is going on in Rome while we are in Philadelphia. This experience is a perfect example of how religious diversity in America works. Serge and I continued to have our own conversation about Christianity and Catholicism whenever we had the time throughout our sojourn in America. I know I will learn much from him and others about the differences between Protestant and Catholic Christians before I return to Saudi Arabia. But first it is important to have a basic understanding of Christianity from a Christian perspective and then some of the perspectives of that same tradition from an Islamic view.

Two thousand years ago, Christianity began as a movement made up primarily of Jews in ancient Palestine. Its founders were disciples of Jesus of Nazareth, who lived roughly between 4 BCE and 37 CE. For Christians, Jesus was born the son of a carpenter and eventually became a well-known religious teacher. As a teacher, Jesus was both respected and controversial. His fame spread throughout the Mediterranean world, where he was known as a powerful miracle-worker and an authoritative teacher. But a number of his teachings were considered offensive by the religious leaders of his Jewish community.

Christians claim that Jesus claimed that God was his "Father," that he said, "I and the Father are one," and that he preached against the hypocrisy that he observed in the religious leaders. He called them "white-washed tombs," claiming that their "outside" was clean but their "inside" was full of decay. According to the Gospel accounts of Jesus' life, the Jewish leaders were driven by jealousy to stop Jesus from teaching. In an attempt to carry out their plans, these leaders put Jesus on trial and declared him guilty of cursing God. They also brought him before the Roman authorities, claiming that Jesus was an insurrectionist who had called himself "King of the Jews." Although the Roman leader Pontius Pilate found Jesus guilty of no crime, he was forced to maintain order by allowing Jesus to be crucified, hung on a cross to die. Three days after his death, the followers of Jesus encountered him alive. Together the life, death, and resurrection of Jesus form the central idea of Christianity. Through his obedience even in death and his vindication in resurrection, Jesus opened up the way for others to live in loving, hope-filled intimacy with God.

For Muslims, Jesus was not crucified. God elevated Jesus to Heaven and a substitute was put on the cross thinking he was Jesus. Muslims also believe that Jesus will come back before the Judgment day and will lead all believers to the right path to Heaven.

As a priest in the Catholic Order of White Fathers in Rwanda, Serge encounters many Muslims. His respect for our differences maximizes how persons seeking faith can be helped to choose a tradition in which to grow and heal. He helped me understand why, for many Catholics and Protestants, evangelism is essential. I have always wondered about the motivations for some Christians when they devote their life to converting non-Christians. I continued to learn from others as well.

The group referred to as "evangelicals" is difficult to pin down, since there is no single portion of Christians that uniquely claims the name. Instead, the term is used to represent a broad-sweeping development, primarily among American Protestants, that has attempted to continue the turn toward respect for the individual begun by Martin Luther in the 16th-Century European Reformation.

The word "evangelical" has its source in the Greek word *euangelion*, which means "gospel" or "good news." Evangelicals were given their name because they had the reputation for wanting to share what they considered "good news." The "good news" is that salvation is available through belief in Jesus. Represented by modern preachers like Billy Graham and Rick Warren, evangelicals preach that humans are sinners and are, therefore, separated from God, who is holy; yet, through the death of Jesus, God provided a way for humans to be forgiven. If they will respond to God's offer of forgiveness by confessing their sins, humans will be brought into a relationship with God and can look forward to being with God in Heaven forever. In other words, evangelicals deem that believing in Jesus is the only way to Heaven, and that those who have not experienced this risen Christ will perish in Hell. This basic desire to make sure everyone finds Heaven as a reward for life on Earth is the motivation for evangelism.

Because of the diverse traditions associated with evangelicalism, the worship practices of these groups vary considerably. Their gatherings are nonetheless united by a few themes: a stress on the individual's personal relationship with God through prayer and songs of worship; an emphasis on sin and the availability of forgiveness through the cross; the centrality of a gospel-oriented sermon; and an opportunity for the individual to respond in faith and obedience.

Until recently, evangelicals have been affiliated with the opinions of American conservatives and most specifically with a pro-life stance on abortion. Evangelicals are united in their belief that life and personhood begins at the moment of conception; hence, abortion is murder. In the last few years, however, a shift has occurred. Represented by figures like Jim Wallis and Brian McClaren, the centrality of the gospel message has been complemented with a concern for the poor, a desire to minimize ecological destruction, and the promotion of world peace.

Perhaps one of the largest Evangelical subgroups is that of the Pentecostals. Deriving their name from an event recorded in the book of Acts, according to which the Holy Spirit descended on the new Christians during the Jewish holiday of Pentecost, the

Pentecostal denominations focus heavily on the inspiration given by the Spirit of God to Christian believers today. Typically, this inspiration is understood as being visibly obvious. Evangelicals believe that the Spirit may encounter individuals by giving them the gift of speaking Heavenly languages, what Christians call "speaking in tongues." Or the Spirit may be encountered in the healing of a sickness or in an enraptured state of ecstasy.

Worldwide, the Pentecostal denomination is growing rapidly. From Myanmar to Mexico, from Australia to Brazil, Pentecostals have seen amazing growth in the last few decades. In Africa alone there are over 41 million Pentecostals, and in the United States there are nearly 60 million adherents out of a total resident population of 307 million.

. . . .

DAY NINE :: SUNDAY
SEPTEMBER 21, 2008

"Let every nation know, whether it wishes us well or ill, that we shall pay any price, bear any burden, meet any hardship, support any friend, oppose any foe, to assure the survival and success of liberty."

—John F. Kennedy, 35th American President, (1917-1963)

This background understanding of Christianity helped prepare our group to meet the African American experience. We met at Mother Bethel Church which is the first African American church in the U.S. It was founded by Richard Allen on June 10, 1794. The story of religious freedom for African Blacks begins with first the need for freedom from slavery and the fight for equality with Whites in the political structures of the country.

On August 20, 1619, Twenty Africans arrived in Jamestown, Virginia, aboard a Dutch ship. They were the first Blacks to be forcibly settled as involuntary laborers in the North American British Colonies, and in 1641, Massachusetts was the first colony to legalize slavery by statute. It is noteworthy that Maryland is recorded as the first state to try to discourage by law the marriage of White women to Black men in 1664. I find it ironically dramatic that we still find judges in Saudi Arabia who would separate a man from his wife and kids because of invisible social ranking. As expected on February 18, 1688, the Quakers of Germantown, PA, passed the first formal antislavery resolution. Vermont was the first state to abolish slavery on July 2, 1777. The 14th Amendment, which made Blacks citizens of the United States, was passed on July 28, 1868, which exemplifies another long and arduous process.

A process that is still not complete, but has come a long way. The '60s of the 20th Century witnessed the most influential movements in the African American story. Martin Luther King, Jr., delivered his "I Have a Dream" speech on August 28, 1963 in the March on Washington which was the largest civil rights demonstration ever. And on March 12, 1964 Malcolm X announced his split from Elijah Muhammad's Nation of Islam. He would be assassinated on February 21, 1965. Not long after that, on April 4, 1968 Martin Luther King, Jr. was assassinated in Memphis Tennessee. Louis Farrakhan, Nation of Islam leader, called for The Million Man March in Washington D.C. on October 16, 1995. The march was described as a call to Black men to take charge in rebuilding their communities and to show more respect for themselves and devotion to their families. It said that over two million men attended the march. Not long after that, on February 25, 2000, Louis Farrakhan announced an end to the 25-year-long rift between the Nation of Islam and the Moslem American Society headed by Wallace Deen Mohammed, who passed away just a few days before my arrival to America. The groups had split in 1975 following the death of Elijah Muhammad.

The year 2008 was a turning point not only in African American history but in world history when Barack Obama received the Democratic nomination for President on June 4, becoming the first Black person in the United States to be nominated for President by a major political party. Obama was then elected the 44th President of the United States and the first Black U.S. President. In his acceptance speech in Chicago's Grant Park later that evening in November, 2008, Obama said, "If there is anyone out there who still doubts that America is a place where all things are possible, who still wonders if the dream of our founders is alive in our time, who still questions the power of our democracy, tonight is your answer."

At six o'clock that day we all were invited to the home of Harry and Kay Halloran; this American couple was so sincere and welcoming. At their house we met with some of their neighbors, including a couple of the Bahai faith and another lovely couple, Mr. and Mrs. John Smith. A story from John connected our countries. When John was eleven years old, he was hospitalized for surgery and next to him was a very old man who told him about his journey to Saudi Arabia where he collected arrowheads that were as old as twelve hundreds years. This man gave John twenty-five of those arrow heads. Last year John met with Prince Turki Alfaisal, the former Saudi Ambassador to the U.S., and presented him five of those arrowheads. Prince Turki, grateful for the gift, promised John to place these arrowheads in one of the royal museums. John asked me where I thought this museum would be; I told him I thought the arrowheads would be at either the Alfaisaliyah Foundation Museum or King Abdulaziz National Museum, both of which are in Riyadh.

39

Harry suggested a style of dialogue in which each one of the guests would take a plate from any of the five tables without knowing who will be at that table, go to the open buffet, then come back to the table and have a dialogue with whoever has arrived. We followed his suggestion and our visit continued long into the night in this gracious atmosphere. Harry, a great businessman, was interested in his youth in religious studies and interfaith activities, but his father asked him to take care of the family business. So he changed his major and built the business, but still holds interfaith dialogue close to his heart. He has established a Chair at Temple University and named it Leonard and Arlene Swidler Interfaith Chair. Kay, Harry's wife, also held a keen interest for intercultural activities. While I was sitting next to her at dinner, I finished my plate and she invited me to go for another round. I did and found a delicious collection of various types of cheese. I love cheese so I picked a piece of each, then I wondered where the cheese fits in the dinner meal. Kay told me that I could eat it whenever I felt like it, and added that Americans, unlike Europeans, are not so particular about the order of food. Later on, she encouraged me to ask her about whatever comes to my mind; Americans also believe that there are no stupid questions.

After dinner I had a lengthy conversation with Sabine O'Hara, the Executive Director of Council for International Exchange of Scholars (CIES). She explained to me how CIES was established. CIES was established in 1946 and is affiliated with 142 countries, but they have only one program with Saudi Arabia which is the Fulbright Program and it had been suspended since 2002 until it was reinstated six months ago. I would be among the first to be in the Program after this suspension.

Sabine mentioned a visit she had with a consultant from the Ministry of Higher Education in Saudi Arabia whose interest was to expand the relationship with the U.S. through their work, expanding the exchanges between the two countries in many subjects and throughout many regions. She commented on how he showed no interest in any collaboration in the areas of History, Religion or the Humanities, claiming that Saudi Arabia did not need exchange in these areas, only in the area of Science. I could not disagree with him more, seeing how, in my experience, most of our educational problems come from that kind of thinking. Those joining us in our conversation agreed that focusing on Science only is nowhere a good plan.

DAY TEN :: MONDAY
September 22, 2008
"We became not a melting pot but a beautiful mosaic. Different people, different beliefs, different yearnings, different hopes, different dreams."
— Jimmy Carter, 39th American President, (1924-)

Mr. Muhammad Modassir Ali joined us today. He is a Muslim from Pakistan, and an Assistant Professor at the International Islamic University Islamabad (IIUI). Mr. Ali is completing a Ph.D. in Comparative Religion at IIUI. His interests include interfaith understanding and Sufism. Mr. Ali has also published "Al-Sumanniyyah" in Al-Dirasat Al-Islamiyyah, and attended the UCSB-Fulbright American Studies Institute Conference in 2003.

Today was Mohammad's first session, so we welcomed him and the members asked him several questions; I simply asked him, "Why are you here?" He explained how one of his professors, a graduate from McGill University in Canada, had encouraged him to participate in this program by applying through the U.S. Embassy in Pakistan. I told Muhammad that although he had told us how he came to the States, he still had not told us why. Then he explained that in his opinion Pakistan and Israel are the only two countries in the world who construct societies based on ideologies. On the other hand, the U.S. is the most secular country in the world, where people have a very open mind and are open for dialogue and he was ready to learn. I just wanted to learn the motivation of a fellow Muslim who came from different background and I felt that I had only a partial answer. Perhaps we would have more time later to talk, but not in front of the whole group.

Our presentation that morning focused on predilection, which is the concept that human development requires a stage in which youth are taught to be like one another and avoid differences in order to create a sense of belonging. We discussed our assumption that children will usually play well together, regardless of color or wealth or prejudice, until taught that to belong to one community, other communities may need to be avoided. Parents will act to teach their children to stay with the people who are from the same race and religion and who hold the same morals and beliefs and keep the children away from those who are different. This predilection must be avoided in my view unless morality is involved. I believe a leader or a parent has the right to draw a boundary if certain moral choices are not honored. Michael claimed that perhaps certain morals are universal and deserved universal application. What then would constitute universal morals? It was clear that no universal morals are agreed upon despite the 1948 UN Declaration of Human Rights. It was also clear that knowing how to raise our children to be interfaith global citizens is difficult.

An example of this difficulty presented itself in the afternoon when the faculty members of the Temple Religion Department were speaking with us. One of the Muslim professors shared the story of how a Christian student told the professor about her interest in his course, but said that she would first have to get permission from her mother. She never came back. The practice of the Religion Department at Temple University to select its faculty with the consideration that each professor of a religious tradition be a practitioner of it will go a long way to building trust between students, their families, and the program.

Professor Zain Abdullah was the only Muslim professor we met during the whole orientation so I was most interested in his syllabus when it arrived a few days before attending his course "Islam in a Global Perspective." The readings for that week were from Mark Levine's, *Heavy Metal Islam*, and Peter Beyer's, *Religion and Globalization*. Professor Zain used these readings to emphasize the different practices between official Islam and popular Islam; the Islamic migrations contributed to this differentiation. Many American academicians and media tend to think that Islamic movements represent grass-roots Muslim societies, while in fact the societies' practices and views are different than those pragmatic movements, such as the Muslim Brotherhood, Wahhabism, and al-Qaeda.

One of the burning issues in the class was about the Islamic Penal Law; for example, how can we use the death penalty with a Muslim who has converted to another religion? And how would that law be applied in a non-Islamic country among a Muslim minority. Professor Zain kindly asked me to comment on this issue, and I stated that the Penal Law is the most complicated part of Islamic Law for Westerners. Then I gave examples of three different penalties related to consuming alcohol, committing adultery and apostasy. I emphasized how Islamic Law intends to protect society. The strict punishment is meant to discourage people from breaking the law, but, in fact, other restrictions on the law mean it is rarely used. In the case of adultery, for example, four witnesses are required before the death penalty may be applied. Because of the private nature of the offense,

42

the death penalty in jurisprudence practice is rarely administered. In other words, this punishment is to prevent the practice of prostitution. The same goes with consuming alcohol, unless someone goes out in public drunk, where he might harm other people, he would not be punished. In fact, in several reports regarding a companion of the Prophet Muhammad, peace be upon him, coming to Omar, the second caliph, to tell him about someone drinking in his home, Omar punished the one who reported it and condemned him for spying on others. In the case of the one who rejects Islam, he harms not only himself but in doing so he insults an entire nation, cursing their religion and honor. The jurisprudence would take the action to prevent this larger harm from happening. In all three cases, the Islamic Law places the good of the society ahead of that of the individual.

When the class was over, a student followed me and wanted to say something so I stopped looked at her and she said "You have nice Puma shoes like mine," I smiled. Honestly, I thought she would have started a more in-depth conversation after such a discussion. While walking back to the hotel, my brother called and I told him about this shoe story; he laughed and said I was lucky she didn't ask me what brand of underwear I was wearing. I laughed too, but later wondered whether what we had learned about predilection might be happening here; that in order to understand the depth of difference I was intimating between her culture and mine, she was actually reaching out first, without realizing it, to reveal how we were alike. Puma sneakers represented a culture we both knew, and from there we might begin our dialogue. This intercultural, interfaith work requires much patience and introspection. We need many more such classes and opportunities to reflect afterward to make a difference.

Chapter 2

"*Always do what you are afraid to do.*"

Ralph Waldo Emerson, AMERICAN POET, (1803-1882)

· · · · · · · · · · · · · · · · · · · ·

DAY ELEVEN :: TUESDAY
SEPTEMBER 23, 2008
"God grants liberty only to those who love it, and are always ready to guard and defend it."
— Daniel Webster, American Statesman, (1782-1852)

At our morning session, Professor Swidler spoke about his book *Jesus was a Feminist: What the Gospels Reveal about His Revolutionary Perspective*. I found his thoughts interesting but overall was surprised that feminism was not more of a phenomenal subject in the American universities I visited, which is what I had expected. I made sure, in any case, to educate myself on basic issues regarding women's studies.

The Women's Rights Movement in America began with the "Declaration of Rights and Sentiments" at Seneca Falls, NY in 1848, developed at the first American Women's Rights Convention. The principal author was Elizabeth Cady Stanton (1815-1902). Stanton, a major reformer, had originally focused her reform efforts on temperance and abolition, but became more committed to women's rights in 1840 after an international abolitionist meeting refused to allow the women delegates to be seated. This act, combined with her dissatisfaction with the degraded lives of the women she saw around her, caused her to devote herself to improving women's lives, legal and economic standing, education, and political rights. Stanton was a brilliant orator and writer, and in 1851, she met Susan B. Anthony (1820-1906). Anthony had already begun working for equal pay for women teachers but was unsuccessful. Stanton and Anthony began collaborating immediately, forming a Women's Temperance Society when they were barred from the men's meetings. Stanton and Anthony lectured and lobbied widely, Stanton often wrote speeches for Anthony when Stanton had to remain at home to care for the children, and Anthony was planning events and projects. In 1869 they founded the National Women's Suffrage Association, a women-only group formed in response to the 14th and 15th Amendments. Stanton and Anthony objected to granting the slaves freed in the Civil War voting rights without also granting them to women. After the Amendments passed, Anthony famously tried to vote on the basis that the Fourteenth had given her the right; she was arrested, found guilty, fined. She never paid. The two also collaborated on the weekly newsletter *Revolution* and the four-volume *History of Women's Suffrage*.

The NAWSA eventually merged with the more moderate American Women's Suffrage Association to form the National American Women's Suffrage Association. In 1912, Alice Paul (1885-1977) joined the NAWSA and began fundraising and organizing member drives to support an equal rights amendment. However, by that time, the NAWSA had turned its focus to state-by-state legislation. State campaigns had

45

been somewhat effective in the western pioneer states, which wanted to attract more women. Paul and Lucy Burns (1879-1966) and their colleagues formed the National Women's Party in 1916 and began employing the techniques used by British women's groups to get results. They aggressively criticized Woodrow Wilson for refusing to pursue women's suffrage, and in 1917 they staged the first demonstration outside the White House, standing silently in front of the gates holding picket signs that demanded the right to vote. Eventually, they were arrested for "obstructing traffic" and were imprisoned at the Occoquan Workhouse, where Paul suffered terrible conditions and abuse. Paul began a hunger strike, joined by many other women and gained the attention of the press. In 1918, Wilson called for Congress to pass legislation to grant women the vote, calling it a "war measure." In 1920, Congress passed the 19th Amendment, granting women the right to vote.

The 72-year period beginning with the "Declaration of Sentiments" and ending with the 19th Amendment is called First-wave feminism. Second-wave feminism, arising after World War II and continuing until today, deals with social inequalities that inhibit women from pursuing careers, like pay differences and the need for childcare; cultural representations and systemic exploitations of women in society, like sexist ideas of women in religion and their segregation in schools and the workplace; and on women's rights over their own sexuality and reproductive capacities, focusing first on contraception and abortion, and now turning towards sexual abuse and rape.

Our discussion of women's rights brought us to a major consideration of what truth is. Professor Swidler has spent his career focusing on "deabsolutizing the truth." This idea basically suggests that a true statement may be true but is not an unlimited truth. For example: "The door is closed." is a true statement but we could also say

First-wave feminism   CHAPTER II

Women Suffrage, the right to vote postal stamp was issued in the United States in 1970. The stamp dispicts suffragettes, 1920, and women voters.

that the door is made of wood and the door is six feet high and so on. Therefore the true statement about the door being closed is subject to six limitations; historicism, intentionality, sociology of knowledge, limitations of languages, hermeneutics, and dialogue. Therefore, if a basic statement like "The door is open." can be viewed in various ways, then more complicated notions like freedom and rights become open to much argument. When the concept of "deabsolutizing the truth" is applied to religious claims about God, serious misunderstandings can occur.

Each member of the group participated in this discussion and tried to explain his or her point of view regarding "the absolute truth." Serge claimed that the understanding of the Trinity in Christianity was an absolute belief for him; yet, although he can express this belief in English and French, he has not been able to find an accurate translation for it in some African languages. Professor Len challenged him even to explain its meaning in English and followed by referring to St. Gregory the Theologian's explanation that the Trinity is not a lie, but a mystery. From an Islamic perspective, both legal and philosophical, there is one absolute truth. Thus Prophet Muhammad, peace be upon him, states that if someone makes an effort to find the absolute truth and he reaches it, then he will be doubly rewarded, but if he does not reach it, then he will be rewarded only once, for his effort. So there is no punishment for the one who fails to reach the absolute truth after trying. So if a Christian, for example, does not arrive at the absolute truth, i.e., Islam, then he or she will not be punished or end up in the Hellfire.

At sunset at 7:00 p.m., we had our Iftar, i.e., breaking of the fast, with the Muslim Students Association (MSA) of Temple University. MSA was established in America in January 1963, and continues to serve Muslim students during their college and university careers by facilitating their efforts to establish, maintain, and develop local MSA chapters. The first MSA was established on the campus of the University of Illinois at Urbana-Champaign by a conference of Muslim students from around the U.S. and Canada. MSA National has been a uniting forum for Muslim students from diverse backgrounds for over four decades. It continues its mission of meeting the needs of Muslim youth on campus with the zeal and energy of the Muslim students. Although it has been influenced and strongly linked with Islamic movements back in the '60s, '70s and '80s it has evolved with a more American identity in recent years, and the members now seem to feel national affinities with the U.S. rather than any affiliation with foreign figures or organizations. This distancing from any non-American Islamic identity keeps them clear of any possible linkage with terrorist organizations.

. . . .

DAY TWELVE :: WEDNESDAY
SEPTEMBER 24, 2008
"Democracy cannot succeed unless those who express their choice are prepared to choose wisely. The real safeguard of democracy, therefore, is education."
— Franklin Roosevelt, 32nd American President, (1882-1945)

This morning, Marsha K., one of the seminar leaders and a Ph.D. student of Professor Len, presented "The Dialogue Decalogue," which contained basic guidelines for constructive interreligious or inter-ideological dialogue. The first rule states that the primary purpose of dialogue is to learn, to change the perception of reality and act upon it. The second is that the interreligious and inter-ideological dialogue must be a two-sided project between two people or two communities. Participants, based on the third rule, must come to the dialogue with complete honesty and sincerity. I find the fourth rule the most important one: that we are obliged to compare our ideals with our partner's ideals, not with their practice. The fifth rule states that each participant must define himself or herself. Then each participant must come to the dialogue with no hard and fast assumptions as to where the points of disagreements are, as stated in rule six. The seventh rule emphasizes equality, stating that dialogue can take place only when participants view one another as equals. In addition, rule eight states that the dialogue can take place only on the basis of mutual trust. The ninth rule states that participants must be self-critical of both themselves and their own religious or ideological traditions. The last, but not least, rule is that each participant must attempt to experience the partner's religion or ideology "from within."

Next, Maria Hornung, also a Ph.D. student of professor Len and member of the Interfaith Center of Philadelphia, began her presentation: Overview of Dialogue Tools. Hornung lecture focused mainly on her book *Encountering Other Faiths*. The purpose of the book and the lecture is to encourage people to know at least one other faith well in any dialogue. This Catholic Sister of Mercy modeled so well the dialogue decalogue in her treatment of participants that we learned as much by how well she listened and engaged us as we did by what she said. We could begin to see ways to respect the "absolute" beliefs that had emerged in the morning. Another Christian perspective helped us understand more this difficult tension between holding to a belief with a clear boundary and yet still respecting the other. Per Faaland, another of Professor Len's students, began by telling us a story from his church. The preacher was working through John's gospel and came upon a passage he described as "important," "powerful," and "a favorite, for its clarity." The preacher began his message by identifying and reading the very familiar verse to them:" Jesus said to them, 'I am the way, and the truth, and the life. No one comes to the Father, but by me'" (John 14.6).

His preacher went on to explain what Per here termed the conventional conservative evangelical interpretation of this verse. The preacher said that they learn from Jesus in this statement that there is no other means of uniting or being with God than to trust in Jesus, and he went on to say that anyone who does not trust in Jesus will be excluded from God's presence. He said that trusting Jesus equals being Christian.

Of course summaries are always unfair. Having admitted that, Per described feeling disturbed as this interpretation didn't sit right with him. Yet still, there it was in the text he regarded as sacred, from the mouth of the one most revered in his religion, and what was he to do? More to the point, what is he to do now? He offered some reflection that occurred to him as he squirmed a bit in that pew at church, and some again as he sat in class listening to Dr. Swidler describe notions that have changed his understanding of truth. With this story, he had given us an example of how "deabsolutizing the truth" has real consequence in how one lives and thinks. Dialogue demands that we reinterpret our faith positions in order to avoid alienating one another; yet, at the same time we want to deepen our understanding of the mystery of God.

At six o'clock we all joined a graduate course, "Theoretical Perspectives in Educational Administration" given by Steven Gross. There were about fifteen students in the class from different departments and various careers. It took about 10 minutes to introduce ourselves to one another. The institution of dialogue provides a great opportunity for the professors from Temple University to visit different countries. One example of that is Professor Gross who visited Indonesia twice, once in the year 2000 and again the following year. This was not as ideal for me, because faculty members of Saudi universities have the opportunity to visit up to three countries each year for research and study. For Professor Gross, "Understanding the Dynamic of Education" is the preferred title for this course.

Our evening session returned to the subject of education with Professor Gross where once again differences in our two systems were discussed. The discussion was cut short, however, by one of the actions that most impressed the Muslim Fulbright participants. The professor excused the Muslim students early in order to break our fast, which we did. This respect and care he showed made us respect him more in turn.

Although fasting for Muslims in America is not that difficult, praying is not as easy as it is in Saudi Arabia. The mosques are very few and one must make a trip to go to the mosque and the prayer time seems to always conflict with either class or work schedules. But, because we have some flexibility around when we may pray, we can usually arrange it in a away that avoids disruption. But this American professor's respect was impressive. Fasting is complicated only at the beginning and the end of Ramadan, i.e., the month of fasting, because of the lunar calendar. Some American Muslims will follow their original country and some will follow their mosque in the U.S., but this issue has been settled recently when most mosques in the U.S. follow the calendar of the Islamic Society of North America (ISNA). ISNA has served the Muslims

New York City

(Left) I wrote, "Hope leads to harmony." Then I posted it to the family members of 9-11 victims.

(Right) I am listening to a story narrated by a victim of 9-11 family member, the World Trade Center can be seen behind me.

in America for well over forty years. During this period ISNA has provided many invaluable services to the Muslim community of North America. Most obvious is the ISNA Annual Convention, a meeting place of people and ideas. In addition to building bridges of understanding and cooperation within the diversity that is Islam in America, ISNA is now playing a pivotal role in extending those bridges to include all people of faith within North America. Young Muslims find the annual convention a place to meet their soul mates; other young Muslim professionals find it a place to network and build their career.

. . . .

DAY THIRTEEN :: THURSDAY
SEPTEMBER 25, 2008
"Every nation in every region now has a decision to make. Either you are with us, or you are with the terrorists."
— George W. Bush Jr., the 43rd American President, (1946-)

Early in the morning we gathered at the Conwell Inn lobby to travel to NYC. It was a nice day, and we got there in time to visit first the Simon Wiesenthal Center. The director of the center started with a short video presentation about the causes of hatred among different nations and religions. Then we saw an exhibition of expressions of racism in the media. At the end of this program we met with the Chief of Civil Society Services from the Outreach Division at the UN. I asked him a question about King Abdullah of Saudi Arabia and how his initiative for dialogue among the civilizations was received. He explained how the idea of dialogue was first initiated by the Prime Minister of Spain in the year 2005, and then was adopted and supported by the Prime Minister of Turkey a few years ago as an "Alliance of Civilizations" to challenge the Samuel Huntington theory of "The Clash of Civilizations." The Saudi proposal is still an ongoing subject discussed at the annual general meeting of the UN that takes place usually in mid-September. Following these other initiatives, he said the Saudi proposal has been received and welcomed globally.

After a short visit to the Religions for Peace Center which seemed to be an ambiguous organization located near the UN, we spent time at Ground Zero, where the 9-11 tragedy took place. I was anxious to see the site of a story that changed the world up close. There was a center run by the victims' families and much construction. Our tour guide told us that they are building four smaller buildings and one skyscraper to replace the World Trade Center. People in the area seemed extremely busy, even distracted to the point that they cannot focus on anything outside the frame of their personal lives. Before leaving, I wrote "hope leads to harmony" and posted it to the family members of the victims.

. . ..

DAY FOURTEEN :: FRIDAY
SEPTEMBER 26, 2008
"Always do what you are afraid to do."
— Ralph Waldo Emerson, American Poet, (1803-1882)

Everyone was tired after the NY trip which resulted in the programs scheduled for the day to be cancelled. We began our day together with Friday prayer at the student center where the MSA chapter meets for Friday prayers. MSA as well as Christian, Jewish and other religious group associations are free to practice their religious activities in the universities; in fact, they receive funds and accreditation for activities that serve good national and international causes. MSA was very active in the early 1970s when Muslims from all over the world started to immigrate to the USA. After the change of immigration regulations in the late '60s, immigration opened up for all countries instead of being limited to European countries. Few Muslims from that era took advantage of the freedom of religious, political, and social organizations to establish organizations; MSA was one of the first. Those pioneer students graduated from universities, became involved in different professional positions and then formed wider national organizations such as the Islamic Society of North America (ISNA) and the Islamic Circle of North America (ICNA), with other more specialized or localized organizations.

There are several common features among these Islamic organizations. I am speaking about the Islamic organizations that I have known for a long time and been involved with, and that is the main reason. Another reason is the difference in time, circumstances, and formation of each organization.

After prayers, we visited Lutheran Theological Seminary in northwest Philadelphia which trains Lutheran pastors. According to the Lutheran World Federation, there are approximately 66 million Lutherans worldwide, nearly half of whom live in Europe.

Today in America, the two largest Lutheran denominations are the Evangelical Lutheran Church in America (ELCA), with over 5 million members, and the Lutheran Church-Missouri Synod (LCMS), with over 2.5 million members. In this visit I began my study of the Lutheran faith.

The fundamental beliefs of Lutherans can be narrowed down to the three "*solas*" that were eventually associated with the Protestant reformation broadly. In Latin these phrases are "*sola scriptura*," "*sola fide*," "*sola gratia*." They mean, respectively, "scripture alone," "faith alone," and "grace alone."

> *Sola Scriptura:* Lutherans maintain that the source of theological truth is not two-pronged, derived from interplay between the teachings of the Bible and the tradition of the church. Because Luther observed a number of abuses stemming from the claim of ecclesial authority, he attempted to drive the church back to its roots, to the scripture upon which its teachings were originally based. Thus, his own method of theological construction was based on a sense of immediacy between himself and the words of scripture, prodding Luther not to assert anything that was contrary to the claims of the Bible. The Bible acted as the final authority over all claims for Christian faith and practice.

> *Sola Fide:* Lutherans maintain that faith alone is the means by which a person is able to attain righteousness before God. On their own, without the aid of Jesus, humans stand before God as sinners. They are guilty of wrongdoing that offends the holiness of God, and they have no ability to claim righteousness before God. Thus, it is only through the very humble posture of faith, belief in the saving power of God, that humans can be made righteous.

> *Sola Gratia:* In response to this faith, the "faith alone" which can save, God declares the guilty person righteous. As a judge looks at a criminal in court, declaring him either guilty or innocent after hearing the evidence, God looks at the sinner who is contrite and humble, who believes that God will forgive those who ask for forgiveness, and God declares that person innocent. Thus, it is God's grace alone, God's free gift of righteousness that can save the individual. There is no mixing of grace and merit, no intermingling of faith and works, in Luther's system. It is only the free gift of God that allows an individual to claim peace with God.

The two biggest Lutheran denominations today in America (ELCA and LCMS) differ on issues related to the ordination of women, the role of scripture in theology, the value of inter-denominational and interreligious dialogue, and the ethics of homosexuality. Yet they are united in their acceptance of these three solas that are used in reference to the teachings of Martin Luther, whose theology formed the foundation of the protestant reformation in general and the Lutheran faith in particular.

We ended the day with the experience that prompted me to choose the quote above for this day. On this Friday, for the Jewish Sabbath, I was invited by Rabbi Marcia Prager to share dinner at her home with her husband Jack and their friends. Jack is also a cantor and musician. It was the first time for me to be in a Jewish home for Sabbath. Together Rabbi Marcia and Cantor Jack led us through a meal and a practice of praise and celebration that involved the story and song of Yahweh which was very moving. The conversation was rich and a true dialogue was happening among the Jews, Muslims, and Christian at the table. I felt I was learning through my experience of this new knowledge which is superior to observation alone.

. . . .

DAY FIFTEEN :: SATURDAY
SEPTEMBER 27, 2008
"What I know for sure is that what you give comes back to you."
— Oprah Winfrey, American media figure, (1954-)

I t is still Ramadan and we have two or three more days left of the fasting period. I joined my host, Pecki Witonsky, and housemate, Ziad, in the kitchen where they were having breakfast. Pecki asked whether I minded their eating while I am fasting. I told her not to worry as I had awakened just before dawn to have some yogurt, bread and water. When they were finished breakfast, Carl went golfing with his son, and Pecki took Ziad and me on a tour of her huge garden. I told her that my dad loved gardening and that his garden was awarded the third best garden in Riyadh. When I walked around I noticed the Japanese style and asked Pecki why this garden made me feel I was in Japan although I had never been in Japan. She said the designer of this garden, indeed, was Japanese and had used a Zen design for the whole garden.

In addition to her love of gardening, Pecki has another special interest that inspired today's quote above. I am fascinated by how many people are interested in the environment in general, and in butterflies in particular throughout North and South America. They track different kinds of butterflies and use websites to follow their movements and migration. Pecki showed me the tiny, light stamp that she puts on the wing of the butterfly. Now if anyone else in America captures this stamped butterfly, that person will know the butterfly passed by this farm in Philadelphia and can record it on his or her website. Jokingly, I told Pecki that if I saw any stamped butterfly in Riyadh I would let her know. She laughed and said not to worry as the butterflies only live for four to six weeks and barely make it to South America. Certainly though, she added, any discovery of an American butterfly in Saudi Arabia would make great news.

Pecki loves to tell her friends about a dream she had after watching the escalation of the second Intifada in Palestine, and how people were again dying in the name of God. She had felt helpless and was pondering, "Where could I find hope for the sons of Abraham?" While pondering this question, she had a dream which she narrates as follows:

"My family and I were living in a desert house, a house we built in the Negev. It was modest, made of desert stone and mud, surrounded with a stone wall. We lived simply and were content. One afternoon friends came to visit. I knew they were going to stay, but where? I turned and looked at the house and saw that new rooms had appeared in the back. I heard 'in my Father's house there are many chambers.' I said, 'I know Jesus is given credit for saying that' and I told myself, the Jewish mystics said that before him. More friends, who I recognize in the dream but not while awake, came and stayed. How would I feed everyone? I looked up on the roof and saw sacks of grain that I did not remember being there. We all lived contentedly. Then I walked into a center courtyard, which I also did not remember, and saw water beginning to spout up in the center of the courtyard. Others joined me. The inside walls of the house dissolved; we all knew we were standing on sacred ground."

Pecki said that when she woke up, still felt a buzz of energy, but didn't understand its meaning. She knew from previous experience that this kind of dream and its vibrations meant something special; but wondered what it could be.

A few days later Pecki went to see her Rabbi to talk about her presentation and also mentioned her dream. Rabbi Marcia Prager smiled and reached for the Torah. She flipped the pages to the section where Hagar, pregnant with Abraham's child, ran away from her mistress Sarah. Hagar was frightened, lost and parched. An angel approached and told her that she would have a son and that his name would be Ishmael and she would go back to Sarai. Hagar then saw a well and named it *Be'er-lahai-roi*, which means The Well of the Living One Who Sees Me. Further in the story, Isaac, son of Sarah, settles near *Be'er-lahai-roi*. Pecki left feeling hopeful and had something to work with, and as she described her awareness, it was different from anything she had ever heard in the past.

The week after 9-11 occurred, Pecki went with her Sufi friend Ayesha to visit Ground Zero and told her about her Torah presentation. Then Ayesha informed Pecki that according to Muslim tradition, Hagar's Well, *ZamZam* is located in Mecca. Pecki's response was, "Your well can be in Mecca and mine in the Negev, but what's the difference? God is the Aquifer."

They talked on about Abraham and about the near sacrifice of Isaac. Ayesha said according to the teachings of Islam, it was Ishmael. Both decided it was time to write a children's picture book focusing on the similarities of our two religions. After all, Abraham was buried peacefully by his two sons Ishmael and Isaac, in the cave in Hebron. It was definitely a time to search for understanding and reconciliation wherever one could find it.

The two stories appeared in one creative book to show the similarities between the two great faith traditions of Judaism and Islam. Her dream had helped produce it and now led to more interfaith involvement. Here in Philadelphia they have an active organization, started by a Jew, a Christian and a Muslim just after 9-11, called Peace Walk. This group organizes an annual interfaith walk through the city to honor the past histories, our present connections, our differences and our combined hope for the future. The similarity of stories and demonstrations of solidarity are important. However, most important to me are the law and lessons. With this same priority, Prophet Muhammad, peace be upon him, allowed his companions and nations to narrate stories from Jewish tradition as long as these stories would not contradict any Islamic law or teaching.

. . . .

DAY SIXTEEN :: SUNDAY
SEPTEMBER 28, 2008
"Baseball gives every American boy a chance to excel, not just to be as good as someone else but to be better than someone else. This is the nature of man and the name of the game."
— Ted Williams, American Baseball Player, (1918-2002).

A shopping day. Pecki drove Ziad and me to the King of Prussia Mall. We are not used to not paying tax on clothing so shopping for our families was fun. When we came back home, Carl was planning to play golf later in the day and shared a conversation about sports in America.

I had played American football once, so I understood the game and enjoy watching it. I have also attended a baseball game between the Yankees and Toronto Blue Jays in Toronto, so I am able to grasp the rules of baseball and find it interesting. I had never thought of watching or playing golf so the conversation with Carl made it interesting. The rules, however, are not that easy, and the rankings are a bit complicated.

Golf is played by trying to hit a small, hard ball into a similarly small hole usually placed between 250 and 690 yards away. A golfer strikes the ball with a special club and tries to navigate the terrain, called a fairway, which may have trees, sand pits, and ponds to trap or deflect the ball. Golfers can bring up to 14 different types of clubs with them to in order to help them hit the ball to varied distances. Fairways do not need to be straight, and accordingly, the golfer may need to use different clubs to move the ball through various sections. Golfers take turns within their party hitting their own balls, and whoever sinks their ball in all eighteen holes with the fewest hits wins. Most competitive golfers earn their money as instructors and occasionally receive money for tournaments. Only a few make money exclusively through competitions. The most famous professional golfer is Eldrick Tont "Tiger" Woods (1975-) who has won fourteen professional tournaments and is currently the #1 golfer in the world. He is famous for his powerful opening swings. For at least a little while, Woods profoundly increased the interest and popularity of golf in America. There are also celebrity golf tournaments, where a professional is paired with an actor, comedian, or music artist, who competes with other teams for charity. These are popular because nothing pleases

Americans more than watching someone, especially someone famous, completely fail. Golf is an elite game, so it is not that popular among the majority of Americans.

Though I had chosen not to go until a later time, others of our group joined one of our seminar leaders, Rebecca Mays, on a visit to the Weavertown Amish Mennonite Church near Lancaster, PA. The Amish are a Christian sect from the Anabaptist tradition, a radical movement arising during the Protestant Reformation. They split from the Mennonites, another Anabaptist sect in 1693, but retain many of the theological doctrines, such as the literal reading of the Bible and repudiation of the government and military. The Amish and the Mennonites emigrated from Europe to William Penn's American colony of Pennsylvania in the 1700s in order to escape persecution.

Amish people rigorously maintain their religious commitment to remaining separate from the world and encouraging humble, simple lives. As a result, the Old Order is most conservative and is thereby known for rejecting modern technology and living much like the early American colonists did. Strict Amish do not use electricity, drive cars, or listen to radio or television. They use gas lamps and ride in horse-drawn buggies. They are also known for their distinctive appearance. Amish men wear black or solid colored clothing, usually long sleeved pants and shirts, plus a hat and coat, and grow long beards, but not mustaches. Amish women wear long, single-colored, long-sleeved dresses, which are dark in color and are covered with a white apron. A white bonnet covers their hair.

The Amish live in large farming communities where they try to support themselves independent of the society around them. Amish families produce their own clothes, food, furniture, and other household items. They usually marry within their community, and have their own schools. Their communities decide for themselves what innovations to adopt, and to what degree; as a result, some Amish are allowed to drive or use electricity, although most retain the distinctive clothing. Because of their unusual mode of life, Americans like to visit the Pennsylvania settlements and purchase handmade goods from the Amish such as quilts and furniture. While the Amish do not like mixing with more worldly Americans, they welcome the opportunity to correct misconceptions about their lives. They are very open to questions and discussions about their religious practice or social life.

When I did get involved in an interfaith dialogue with the Amish on a subsequent trip to America, I found them very open, very straight forward, and very honest about their beliefs which were very far from my own beliefs because of their strong belief in the Trinity. I highly respect the Amish, and admire the way they engage in dialogue, but I met with more progressive members and wonder whether the more conservative Amish or Mennonites would even have entertained the idea of interfaith dialogue.

57

. . . .

DAY SEVENTEEN :: MONDAY
SEPTEMBER 29, 2008
"We change, whether we like it or not."
— Ralph Waldo Emerson, American Poet, (1803-1882)

Zainab Al-Zuwaij is Co-founder and Executive Director of the American Islamic Congress (AIC). In her session with us, she talked about the establishment of the AIC right after 9-11. Their programs include: a Capitol Hill distinguished speaker series; panels on Muslim affairs for Congress; Project Nur (which means light in Arabic) that promotes student leadership and activism at college campuses; and public education forums on interfaith dialogue and advice for responding to hate speech. They collaborate with several other Muslim organizations: Hands Across the Mideast Support Alliance, (HAMSA), to aid civil rights reformers; the Muslim Interfaith Council to focus on building bridges without baggage via open dialogue; and the Pledge for Iraq to empower female civic leaders and civil society via grants and training.

Muhammad Ali asked how Zainab was using the term "radicalism" in her talk. She stated that once a person's practice of religion harmed another human being, then that person's faith had crossed a boundary into radicalism. Radicalism could be found in any religion, she claimed. Muhammad's second question was about the Iraq situation and her views of the American invasion. Zainab briefly commented on the situation before and after Saddam explaining that, from her point of view, all Iraqis admired the American invasion. Some of us questioned the accuracy of her statement which leads us to discuss the credibility of AIC among Muslims. Ziad wondered why the AIC focuses on events outside America when there is a great deal of need for the dialogue among Muslims and Americans inside America. Zainab agreed with him but did not really bring a clear answer to justify what we saw to be neglected.

Another confusion was the relationship between AIC and the Council for American Islamic Relations (CAIR). I had thought that they collaborated, but as Zainab explained, CAIR's mission is to enhance understanding of Islam, encourage dialogue, protect civil liberties, empower American Muslims, and build coalitions that promote justice and mutual understanding inside the U.S. So their activities are quite different from AIC. Moreover, there is no collaboration between the two organizations.

. . ..

DAY EIGHTEEN :: TUESDAY
SEPTEMBER 30, 2008
"With the new day comes new strength and new thoughts."
— Eleanor Roosevelt, American First Lady, (1884-1962)

On this day Jews celebrate *Rosh Hashanah*, (the New Year) which is not fixed on one day of the Gregorian Calendar because it is in accordance with the Jewish calendar, for example, next year Rosh Hashanah is on September 18. In the Rosh Hashanah prayers Jews say, "This is the day of the beginning of Creation." As the new moon of Tishre rises and divine desire increases further. On Rosh Hashanah Jews re-link their souls to God's creative will, God's desire to emanate goodness into the unfolding creation.

In most of the Jewish holidays, I joined Marcia Pager and her husband Jack either at their synagogue or their home. Their synagogue is typical in some ways and very unusual in others. There is a great deal of freedom to explore religious traditions there, and to celebrate in ways that link ancient traditions to modern sensibilities and needs. For instance, in Philadelphia it is possible to find synagogues that are attempting to be very true to a traditional style of religious practice that links members to particular geographic regions in which a particular style of strong religious intensity made a very deep impression.

So there are synagogues of diverse Hasidic styles, which carry forward traditions from the Ukraine, Russia and from elsewhere in Eastern Europe. There are Sephardic synagogues that carry forward the legacy of the Spanish and Turkish Jewish communities. There are Mizrachi congregations whose members carry forward a legacy of Jewish prayer practice from the Arabic countries. But there are variations in style even among these, from very traditional to more contemporary in outlook. There are also synagogues which are modern orthodox, whose members wish to live within a highly traditional lifestyle but not one particularly linked to any specific geographic area of Jewish settlement, but to a generally Northern European/American approach to being a modern person with a good secular education while still making a strong commitment to orthodox interpretations of Jewish law.

Then there are the major denominations which are highly-organized and spread across the nation. Conservative Judaism was known as Historical Critical Judaism in Europe, meaning it absorbed the legitimacy of scientific and historical research, linguistic research, anthropological research, et cetera, into its understanding of Jewish text, law and practice, and made significant modifications to how texts and Jewish law should be understood. This is one of the liberal movements of Jewish life, but still very much rooted in a rabbinic process for the interpretation of Jewish law.

Reform Judaism has its roots in Europe as well, very radically changing the approach to Jewish life based on the European experience of the Enlightenment. This movement adopted some theological approaches and stylistic changes that echoed strong trends in the Protestant Christian world at the time, and those approaches are only slowly being influenced back towards some more traditional approaches. It has become well-known for championing the ethical teachings of the prophets and emphasizing social justice and ethics over ritual and law and made personal choice a primary criterion for adhering to ritual practices.

Reconstructionist Judaism emerged in the 1930s as an intellectual trend within the U.S.-based Conservative Judaism and then split to form a new denomination. It pioneered the full equality of women and embraced a variety of "process-theology" in its way of understanding God as a force or process that moves through the natural world which causes humans to strive for moral excellence and the highest good. Many changes in the liturgy were made to eliminate a supernatural depiction of God. Reconstructionist Judaism also challenges the assumption of top-down authority of the rabbis and urges congregational life to be based on a high level of education and democratic choices.

This synagogue where Marcia and Jack attend falls into a style that is often called "Jewish Renewal." It is a modern phenomenon that results from the blend of diverse streams of Jewish practice. Renewal has similarities to all the approaches mentioned above, and differences from each. Renewal blends a very deep grounding in traditional approaches to understanding Jewish life and practice, and particularly a deep appreciation for the spiritual wisdom of the Hasidic and mystical approaches, but brings these into the contemporary life. Jewish Renewal is the ongoing creative project of a generation of Jews who are seeking to renew Judaism and bring its spiritual and ethical vitality into today's lives and communities while embracing a global vision of the role of all human beings.

We had the opportunity to visit the Arch Street meetinghouse. A large group of Quakers gather every Sunday inside the meetinghouse, which is their place of worship. They sit quietly, side-by-side on simple benches with backs without music or a pastor. They trust the biblical citation that says God is found most in sheer silence. They wait upon God to speak through someone present who will stand to deliver a message or ministry that that person believes is for the nurture, solace, or edification of all present.

Their worship extends through the week in showing loving concern for one another's well-being in daily life. During the hour of worship, others may speak as well, but rarely do more than three or four speak. The worship concludes with the shaking of hands and sharing of news among community members.

This open form of worship grew out of the protestant reformation on the continent in 17th Century England. Rural farmers and village merchants began to hold these simple worship gatherings with the belief that the Spirit of God reveals truth and love through the act of opening one's heart in active waiting and therefore has no need for music, icons, or appointed clergy to receive the holy word. The meditative or contemplative silence awaiting the inward teaching of Jesus takes the place of an outward liturgical service. This worship then leads one to live what Quakers call a "sacramental life."

A sacrament is "an outward sign of an invisible grace" from God. Quakers live out testimonies in their daily life as sacraments. The primary testimonies include peace, sustainability, and integrity. From these come the testimonies of harmony, equality, simplicity, and community. In practice, these testimonies mean most Quakers do not participate in armed conflict, they respect men and women as equals, they eat low on the food chain, live "green," do not swear or take oaths, dress modestly, give generously to the poor, infirm, and elderly, and trust that "there is that of God in everyone."

. . ..

DAY NINETEEN :: WEDNESDAY
OCTOBER 1, 2008

"A great many people think they are thinking when they are merely rearranging their prejudices."

— William James, American psychologist and philosopher, (1842-1910)

Today is Eid al-Fitr, in which Muslims celebrate their completion of the fast during the month of Ramadan; Muslims give a special donation for Eid al-Fitr which may be buying a dress for a poor person, or feeding them that day. Also, most of them pay their alms tax (zakat) which is about 2.5 % of their total net savings for one calendar year which is distributed to the poor.

We went to pray the Eid prayer at a Sufi mosque, the Guru Bawa Muhaiyaddeen Mosque in West Philadelphia. Sufism started in the United States around the time of the World Parliament of Religions in 1893. Following that time, the first major Sufi teacher was Hazrat Inayat Khan (1882-1927) who came from India on tour as a Hindustani musician and then began spreading the teachings of the Chishti Sufi Order in both America and Europe.

After Inayat Khan, Sufi influence was fairly limited. For one thing, there was not a strong Muslim presence in the U.S. until after the change in the immigration laws of

1963, which opened immigration to larger numbers of non-Europeans. Around the same time, the counter-culture movement of the 1960s and concomitant interest in eastern spirituality revived interest in the Inayat Khan movement. His son, Pir Vilayat Khan, revived the movement in the 1960s under the name "Sufi Order in the West" or the "Message in our Time." At present, the name is "Sufi Order International" as reflects the more transnational currents of our time. Today Inayat Khan's grandson, Zia Inayat Khan, has been invested with the succession of the Order and conducts teachings from his base.

In the U.S. today, there are roughly three types of Sufi movements; New Age, Shari'a-focused, and traditional. The New Age strand is more universal in outlook and invokes Sufism and aspects of Muslim tradition as inspirations without demanding that adherents formally convert to Islam. Included here are the Sufi Order International, the Society for Sufi Studies (Idreis and Omar Ali Shah), and the Dances of Universal Peace Movement.

Other Orders, mainly recruiting Americans, are grounded in the Islamic *shari'a* (ritual law) and see being Muslim as essential to spiritual progress within the Sufi tradition. Most of the leaders of these movements are immigrants from Muslim societies.

Finally, there are pockets of immigrants from Muslim societies, particularly in larger urban centers such as New York, Chicago, and Los Angeles who follow Sufism in ways very similar to practices in their home societies. Adaptations of Sufi ritual and institutions to the American context include practices such as the visitation of the shrines of departed saints (*awliya*) and a more accommodating attitude to the presence and participation of females. The traditional Sufi practice of pilgrimage to the tombs or shrines of departed Sufis has been transplanted to the American context as the first generation of leadership including Murshid Samuel Lewis (New Mexico), Guru Bawa (Pennsylvania), and Shah Maghsoud (California) has been memorialized on American soil.

The constituencies and membership of these various American Sufi movements vary because they represent diverse religious and social orientations. The Sufi Order in the West and the Idries Shah Movement have had a broader impact on mainstream American culture due to their publishing activities and outreach to other communities through transpersonal psychology, holistic health, and Sufi dancing. Interest in these movements probably peaked in the mid 1970s. While the Sufi Order claims 10,000 member initiations with Pir Vilayat Khan, many more Americans have attended Sufi seminars, camps, or read publications.

Sufism is practiced in both the Shi'i and Sunni branches of Islam but had a proportionately smaller impact among African American Muslims although some interest has been sparked by activities of the Tijaniyya, an Africa-based Order, and by the Naqshbandi-Haqqani Order, which probably has the most diverse following among the Sufi orders in the United States.

DAY TWENTY :: THURSDAY
OCTOBER 2, 2008

"Death is not the greatest loss in life. The greatest loss is what dies inside us while we live."
— Norman Cousins, American Political Journalist, (1915-1990)

T oday we heard the sad news of the death of a friend of one of our seminar leaders, Racelle. He was physicist. Our group is becoming like one family in our caring for what happens to each of us personally outside our sessions together.
Our first session today was lead by Howard Cohen who introduced Halloran Philanthropies. He helped us see the influential connections between business and interreligious dialogue as well understand the philanthropic work of our hosts of the previous week, Harry and Kay Halloran. The logo of the Harry Halloran institution has a big letter "H" representing the light; underneath it there is a path that leads to the sun on the top of the "H." An interesting story is related to this logo. When Benjamin Franklin walked up to the desk in Philadelphia's Independence Hall to sign the American Constitution, he saw the half sun carved into the back of the chair behind the desk. He spoke to his colleagues, wondering whether the sun was rising or setting given the unknown consequences of their action. So it is for each one of us in every major step of our lives; we could ask, "Is the sun rising or setting at this stage?" Logos are not just trademarks but they have deep meaning and sometimes history within them.

Julie Sheetz-Willard followed with a presentation of the history of the Dialogue Institute, beginning with the founding of the *Journal of Ecumenical Studies (JES)* by Professor Len, and his wife, scholar Arlene Swidler, and Nancy Krody, who has been the journal's managing editor for over thirty years. In the past few years, Harry Halloran has helped the *JES* to start the Dialogue Institute to do interreligious dialogue training seminars, consult with businesses globally, provide resource material for a network of dialogue initiatives through a web presence and to further global interreligious and intercultural dialogue in general. These efforts are the outgrowth of the scholarly trialogues that the *JES* has organized for decades. Establishing an institute or non-profit organization, generally speaking, is a very easy process in America once the purpose and objectives are clear and valuable. This accessibility explains the tremendous number of American organizations and foundations locally and all over the world that support, offer, and participate in good causes.

. . ..

DAY TWENTY ONE :: FRIDAY
OCTOBER 3, 2008

"I've lived in Europe for the better part of twenty years, and I've noticed that one of the biggest errors Europeans make is to dismiss America as having no culture. That's an incredible mistake, and whether it's born of arrogance or neurosis, it's wrong."

— John Malkovich, American Actor, (1953-)

At 6:00 a.m., I went downstairs to the hotel lobby to say goodbye to the first group leaving Philadelphia. Fatima was going to Seattle, Mousse to Houston, Muhammad Ali to Detroit, and Wasey to Connecticut. Ziad was there to say goodbye to them as well. Ziad, Ghassan, and I are supposed to leave the hotel at 9 am; Ziad to NY, Ghassan to Washington D.C. and me to Chicago. Mehri was the only one staying in Philadelphia. In those three weeks we built a very strong relationship and trust among us and everyone was certain that our friendships would be long-lasting. We looked forward to reconvening in Denver halfway through our sojourn and then again in Washington, D. C. just before we would return to our home countries.

William French called to confirm our rendezvous at the airport. Traveling by airplane in the U.S. after 9-11 is a hassle. Americans and foreigners have to undergo multiple security screenings: travelers are not allowed to carry any liquid, must remove shoes and belts, uncase computers, and there are even signs stating that it is prohibited to joke about any of the previous issues. People have grown accustomed to these procedures and come early to the airport to avoid delays.

Although Chicago O'Hare International Airport is one of the largest airports in the U.S., it was very easy to find my way to the baggage claim where I met William, a most kind and caring person. I asked him whether I should call him William or French; he said, "You can call me Bill." I remembered a person named William from Florida who is known by his nickname Bill. William told me about different nicknames in the U.S., for example, the nickname for William is always Bill even though there is no connection between the two names. The nickname for Richard is Dick like Dick Cheney, the Vice President. Sometimes there is a connection like a shorter version of the name, for example, Christopher is usually shortened to Chris.

I immediately noticed differences between Chicago and Philadelphia. The United States is a large country, but it has several cultural regions that can be loosely characterize in different ways. The major regions are the East Coast, the South, the Midwest, and the West.

The East Coast is made of the states along the East coast, but only above the upper half of Virginia extending to the middle of Pennsylvania and continuing up to Maine. It includes cities like Boston, New York, Philadelphia, Richmond, and Washington, D.C.

63

The region is highly-urbanized and industrial, and contains several of the best American universities, like Harvard, Princeton, and Yale. The area tends to be liberal politically, consistently voting Democrat, with the exception of Rhode Island; and due to their large cities, they have a very diverse immigrant population. New England is known for seafood, especially clams, oysters, and lobster. Maryland is also known for lobster and there is the famous National Aquarium in its capital, Baltimore.

The South is made up of the southern half of Virginia extending south along the coast to Florida, along the Gulf Coast to Texas and then north to Kentucky and Tennessee. The South is made up mostly of rural and agricultural areas; famous Southern crops are Georgia peaches and Florida oranges, and until recently, Southern cash crops were cotton and tobacco. Major Southern cities include New Orleans, Atlanta, Nashville, and Columbia. Although the South was previously Democrat, they have become heavily Republican and politically conservative. The South is very proud of its culture and traditions, like hunting, land-owning, and biblical values. That tradition often includes the Confederacy, and the majority White population gives the South a reputation for racism. Southern food includes a lot of pork: sausage, bacon, ham, and pork chops are favorites, along with various fried foods, like fried chicken, fried greens, and fried apples. The South even developed a method for frying turkeys whole, although they occasionally explode. Other famous Southern foods include: grits, ground corn boiled into a porridge that is usually mixed with butter.

Texas and Florida are both part of the South, but have slightly different cultures. Florida is a major vacation and retirement spot, and has a large Cuban population. Florida is the home of Disneyland and the beaches of Miami. It is also sharply divided politically, making it a swing state. Texas is one of the largest states, and unlike other Southern states, has a large cattle and oil industry. They also have two of the largest cities, Houston and Dallas. Texans are exceptionally proud of their state, wearing leather boots, large Texas hats, and bragging about how great Texas is, even years after they move away. I can't forget a moment in Philadelphia when I was talking with some friends about American culture compared to European culture. Suddenly a Texan came up to us to say, "I am from Texas and I am here to welcome ya!" How did I know? His dress and his accent were unmistakable.

The Midwest is made up of several states in the middle and north of the country: from Ohio west to Kansas, and then north to North Dakota. The southwestern and eastern parts of the Midwest are generally rural and focus on agriculture, which provides most of the country's corn. The states near the Great Lakes have major cities like Chicago and Detroit, as well as more industrial economies such as the automotive industry. People in the Midwest are considered to have conservative Catholic or Lutheran values, but are more private about religion, unlike the South, which is very public about its Protestant Christianity. The region is divided politically: states like Kansas and the Dakotas are mostly Republican, while Illinois is securely Democratic; Ohio, however, was a swing state in the 2004 and 2008 elections. The Midwest is a very musically-creative area. Chicago is famous for Jazz and Blues, and Cleveland, Ohio, is considered the home of Rock 'n' Roll. If you have a taste for Jazz and happen to be in Chicago, you should not miss the opportunity to go to one of the historical Jazz and Blues sites. Midwesterners frequently eat what is called American food: beef and pork, particularly hamburgers and hot dogs, potatoes, bread, cheese, milk, and corn. Iowa produces the most corn of any state; the main reason politicians support ethanol research is because Iowa holds its Presidential primaries first. A notable exception is Chicago, which is one of the most diverse cities in the United States, and offers all kinds of cuisine, even if its citizens eat mostly sausage and pizza.

The West is the largest region, containing everything west of Texas and the Dakotas. The region is very diverse geographically whereas the East and South are mostly mountainous and the Midwest is virtually flat. The West contains the Rocky Mountains, the prairies, deserts, and rainforests. California even sits on a major geological fault line, prompting many Republicans to jokingly pray that it falls into the ocean. It shows a cultural distinction similar to the Midwest. The more rural sections are near the center of the country, and they tend to be conservative and Republican. Utah, for example, is populated mostly by Mormons, who have very conservative religious views. On the other hand, the influx of immigrants from Latin America have begun to shift the border states more toward the Democratic party, while still remaining socially conservative. California is the most divided politically; its large cities, especially Los Angeles, tend to be heavily, almost fanatically Democratic and liberal, while other areas are moderate Republican. The Western economy has a large agricultural base, especially cattle, wheat, and local specialties like Washington apples and Idaho potatoes. The coastal states have a large technological and computer industry, with Microsoft and Boeing both in Washington and Silicon Valley in California. Los Angeles also contains Hollywood, the center of the American movie industry.

Westerners eat different foods: states along the southern border eat modified Mexican food, including larger portions of meat; northwestern states eat steak and chili with local vegetables; Washingtonians eat salmon and local vegetables, along with various Asian recipes. California introduced both Chinese food and Japanese sushi to America, and Los Angeles offers some of the best dining in the world. Once I was undecided on what to order, and a friend of mine who travels a lot from coast to coast told me that the best thing to order is seafood on the East and West Coasts, and steak and vegetables in Midwest. If you are in Philadelphia you must have Philly cheese steak at Pat's King of Steaks. They even have a sign that says "Don't eat a misteak" which refers to its chief rival, Geno's Steaks. In NY, you must have a hotdog at Times Square. In VA, try chicken kabob at Duke Kabab on Little River Turnpike.

. .. .

DAY TWENTY TWO :: SATURDAY
OCTOBER 4, 2008
"An Englishman is a person who does things because they have been done before.
An American is a person who does things because they haven't been done before."
— Mark Twain, American Writer, (1835-1910)

Today I was settling down in my new apartment in Evanston, Illinois, and getting to know my neighborhood, the transportation, and stores. I spent the rest of my day watching some TV shows. The shared events, names, and news that make up American popular culture are centered largely on television. Popular television shows, hot stories on news networks, and blockbuster releases provide Americans with the frame of reference that they use to make ordinary conversation and connect with co-workers and acquaintances. For example, large numbers of American women of a certain age who know nothing about each other can discuss Oprah Winfrey (1954-). The star of "The Oprah Winfrey Show," Oprah, whom everyone calls by her first name, overcame a difficult childhood and started a local talk show that has grown to international fame with her intimate interview style and vulnerable open discussion of her life. She regularly affects the purchasing habits of her audience, telling them about her new favorite soap or pillowcase, and most famously, the newest book in the Oprah Book Club. She also informs the spiritual outlook of her viewers by sharing the lessons that have helped her to achieve happiness. American pop culture is made up largely of images, characters, and stories from shows like Oprah where a large audience follows the show with avid attention.

A major facet of American pop culture are celebrities, mostly actors and musicians, but also some writers, artists, corporate leaders, and politicians. Entire magazines, television shows, and network channels, and websites are dedicated to providing virtually any fact about the lives of celebrities: their new projects, their private lives, what they are wearing, addictions, tantrums, anything. Britney Spears (1981-), for example, is an American pop singer who became famous as a teenager for her fun upbeat songs. Seeing the movie about her biography explained to me the purity of her mind and life. She was so vivid and her personal life was so clear and compelling to everyone that she made everyone love her. Ironically, this attention was also her undoing. As her fame increased, she became more widely known for her greatly sexualized image, her glamorous relationship with pop star Justin Timberlake, her significantly less glamorous relationship and eventual marriage to backup dancer Kevin Federline, and her pregnancies rather than her music.

As the Internet gains popularity, websites, blogs, and videos are becoming a significant source of popular culture. The Internet is as influential as television for the new generation. AOL and more recently Facebook are examples of the new trend for young Americans to use the Internet. Another show I like to watch is America's Got

Talent. Hundreds of people, young and old, in groups or as individuals, will line up to show their talents in their hope of becoming a celebrity.

The "American Dream" refers to what Americans feel is a distinctly American story: responsible, hardworking people dedicate themselves to their vocation — sweat and sacrifice—and through their talents and efforts elevate themselves to acclamation and personal success. Many American movies and novels depict poor, deprived and unfortunate individuals raising themselves up from poverty and low-paying, menial jobs to high-paying careers and a luxurious lifestyle as a reward for their labors, a plot often called the "rags to riches" story. This vision reflects numerous American values, like the Puritan values inherited from the Pilgrims, equality of opportunity, and the value of capitalism.

Although far from a reality, Americans work for every citizen to enjoy an equality of opportunity, that is, to ensure that everyone has the same opportunity to achieve their dreams and aspirations starting out. Anyone of any race, gender, or religion should have the same opportunities as everyone else, and be rewarded solely on the basis of their merit and work. Americans have passed anti-discrimination laws and instituted programs like Affirmative Action to help overcome longstanding prejudices and underlying inequalities to make this a reality.

Where the law fails, Americans hope that capitalism will make up the difference. One of the reasons that Americans are so devoted to capitalism is that they believe that, as an economic system, it rewards excellence despite other obstacles. For example, despite enormous racial prejudice, Black music artists have been able to find international fame through Jazz, Rhythm and Blues, and Hip-hop. Although these stories are often the exception for underprivileged Black communities, Americans take their success as an expression of capitalism's power to recognize and promote worthy contributions. More and more however, Americans are admitting that even if free markets under equal conditions would encourage and reward the best, conditions are far from genuinely equal.

. . ..

DAY TWENTY THREE :: SUNDAY
OCTOBER 5, 2008
"How far can you go without destroying from within what you are trying to defend from without?"
— Dwight Eisenhower, 34th American President, (1890-1969)

I am on a flight to NYC where I will attend meetings with the Steering Committee for the Second International Conference on Dialogue of Civilization, arranged by Florida State University and the Alliance of Civilizations at the UN. The establishment of this UN Alliance of Civilizations is credited to Juan Carlos, the Prime Minister of Spain, and his initiative in 2005 to build bridges and encourage dialogue among civilizations. The following year, the initiative was supported by the Prime

Minister of Turkey after which the UN started the UN Alliance of Civilizations Program.

I arrived in NYC a day ahead of the meetings to visit friends. I had been here before, but on the streets I was reminded how one cannot feel lonely in this city because of all the people. I called my old friend and invited her and my new friend, Ziad, to go to dinner. On our way to the restaurant I noticed so many dogs; it would seem that almost one-third of New Yorkers walk with dogs. As usual, I couldn't resist asking a New Yorker who happened to be walking beside me about this matter: "Why does everyone walk with a dog?" He stopped walking, looked at me, and said that he himself had a German Shepherd, one of those big dogs that you do not want to mess with or even get close to. Then he said, "Do you know why people in NY have dogs?" I said, "No, please explain." "Trust and communication," he said. "Yeah," he adds, "in NY you cannot communicate with humans anymore, no humanity is left in the city, and that's why people communicate and live with dogs." I thanked him, wished him luck and suggested he not give up on humans. He said "No, not in the city." Then we had to go in different directions. I understood better the miserable situation New Yorkers have; even many people walking side by side might still feel lonely. They can defend their beautiful "Big Apple" and yet from within have lost something important. So the dogs become very important. Americans take care of dogs like they take care of their own kids, feeding them, cleaning them, walking them, and even sometimes dressing them.

My New Yorker friend suggested a nice place on St. Mark Street for dinner as she does not like to go to tourist places like Times Square where it is crowded and expensive for nothing. After we had dinner, Ziad and I went to see Times Square and it was just as she described. In addition, many New York Police Department (NYPD) officers walking the streets reminded us of the high crime rate in the city. I was grateful to have real friends in New York.

. .. .

DAY TWENTY FOUR :: MONDAY
OCTOBER 6, 2008

"America was the land of education and opportunity. It was a new land to which all people who had youth and a youthful mind turned."

— Claude McKay, American Poet, (1889-1948)

Today was the first meeting for the Steering Committee of the Second International Conference on the Dialogue among Civilizations. As I had had some work to do during some of the meetings, I asked Kristen Puts to lend me her notes, telling her I might use them in my journal. She smiled and reminded me to give her credit if I used her work. Usually, in my side of the world, people would say the opposite, "You can use my notes, but please don't mention my name." I find that ironic. Her notes were very detailed so I have only summarized the important themes of the meeting which included the following: the first topic was economics and development which included a discussion of how religious institutions affect economic values. Are conflicts based on religion or economics? How does globalization increase these conflicts? The second topic was human rights. How do we educate for human rights? How do we reach out to other partners and educational institutions? How can we teach students about human rights through actions and experiences with other countries and cultures? The third topic was media. How do we use the interactive media as a new forum for these dialogues? What is the role that media plays in perpetuating stereotypes and unhelpful notions of "the other?" The fourth topic was migration. What is the percentage of the world's population who live outside of their native country? How do nations deal with immigrant integration? What policies and programs do governments put into place to assimilate new immigrants? How do we bring together scholars who are just beginning to look at immigrant integration? Sabine O'Hara, from CIES, who was born in Germany and become an American citizen, raised an essential point, reminding us of the difference between education and learning, and that we should pay attention to both.

Immigrants play an important role in America. They are professors at universities, scholars at research centers and labs, farmers on farms, and laborers in industrial factories, businesspeople. One can find them in every productive spot in America; they are part of the great American heritage, culture, and future. Their role in this dialogue could make a big difference.

. . . .

DAY TWENTY FIVE :: TUESDAY
OCTOBER 7, 2008
"A single conversation across the table with a wise man is better than ten years mere study of books."
— Henry Wadsworth Longfellow, American Poet, (1807-1882)

The best relationship you can build between individuals from diverse cultures is one built on trust. Trust is established over time through interaction. Omar, the second caliph, stated that you get to know men by one of three means; by traveling with them, by trading with them, or by being their neighbors. This short trip to NY where I met with Len revealed his character, and I feel comfortable to describe him as a devoted religious man, and I intentionally said "devoted religious" rather than "devoted Christian" because he has devoted his life for the purpose of all religions despite the religions' origins. In his final stage of his career he has become more of a global person which we all should be to serve humanitarian causes. Unfortunately, religious and political policies which should be used to spread peace and protect human rights are used to spread fear and annihilate human rights.

There are hundreds of people like Len around the world, one just has to find them and stand with them in support of their causes. Standing up and praising is not enough, but we have to work together and all take the high road which is not going to be easy.

Chapter 3

"*If a nation expects to be ignorant and free, it expects what never was and never will be. ...When the press is free and every man can read, all is safe.*"

Thomas Jefferson, 3RD AMERICAN PRESIDENT, (1743-1826)

. . . .

DAY TWENTY SIX :: WEDNESDAY
OCTOBER 8, 2008
"Stand with anybody that stands right. Stand with him while he is right and part with him when he goes wrong."

— Abraham Lincoln, 16th American President, (1809-1865)

Back in Illinois, I was introduced to a few faculty members of the Loyola Ethics Department. A most informative and inspiring professor was Aana Vigen. Her friendly attitude and strong social and scholarly involvement in different topics interested me, topics such as environment from a religious Christian perspective, the history of Christian religious movements, and current political and social issues. She was kind to answer my questions and to lend me several sources from her library or from the Loyola Library that are related to my questions.

My conversation with Aana took many different paths, including learning more of the origin of Lutherans and the Protestant Reformation. I realized I could not learn much without knowing more about Martin Luther (1483-1546).

No other Christian has influenced Protestant Christianity as much as Martin Luther. Fueled simultaneously by a passion for Christian Scripture and a hatred for ecclesiastical abuses, Luther began a movement that would later become known as the Protestant Reformation, a movement that would essentially split the worldwide church.

At the age of 22, after being trained as a lawyer, Martin Luther was traveling, when a terrible thunderstorm hit. Being scared for his life, Luther cried out in agony, "Help me St. Anne, and I will become a monk!" This "vow" to God through St. Anne resulted in Luther taking vows as a monk. He joined an Augustinian monastery and in due time ended up as a teacher of the Christian Bible at the University in Wittenberg, Germany.

As a leader in the Christian church, Luther observed abuses of power carried out by other leaders in the church. After preaching against these practices, Luther, especially over the issues of selling indulgences, made his disagreements public. Those who bought these indulgences were promised reduced punishment for their own sins and for the sins of their loved ones. He publicized his disagreement with this practice on October 31, 1517, by nailing his famous "Ninety-Five Theses" to the door of the Castle Church in Wittenberg, a place where public announcements were regularly placed.

After being excommunicated, or kicked out of the church, in 1521, Luther was ordered to appear before a general assembly of the Roman Empire, a group called the "Diet of Worms." He was accused of heresy, incorrect teaching, and was commanded

71

to recant. But, Luther insisted that he could not change his views, unless he was convinced by others that his understanding of Christian scripture was incorrect. As no one was ever able to convince him otherwise, Luther did not change his position. In a climactic display of conscientious objection, Luther said, "I cannot and will not recant anything, for to go against conscience is neither right nor safe. Here I stand; I can do no other, so help me God."

Being in a position against the mainstream religious leaders is not a favorable experience. It is not the right place to tell stories of Muslim scholars who went against the mainstream and how they were abandoned. But from my own experience, I conclude that once one is confident and honest in following the righteous path, then no matter how people stand against him or her, that person will have meaningful influence and great outcomes.

Although he was arrested, Luther was eventually kidnapped by friends, who placed him in hiding. During this time Luther worked many long hours to translate the Christian Bible from its original wording in Hebrew and Greek into the German vernacular of his day. He believed that the commoner had as much right to understand the words of Scripture as the theologian, motivating him to stay faithful to this very difficult task.

Although during the remainder of his life, Luther faced threats from fellow Protestants and Catholic leaders, he remained faithful to his understanding of the gospel, the good news that God could graciously make sinners righteous through their faith. He organized Christian schools, wrote instructions for Christian teachers, composed hymns, wrote commentaries on Christian scripture, and taught regularly from the Bible.

After Martin Luther initiated the Protestant Reformation by expressing his disapproval with many ecclesial practices, other theologians attempted to help Luther's nascent theology blossom into a mature understanding of Christianity. One of the most important theologians who went about this task was the Swiss reformer, John Calvin (1509-1564). Calvin's ability to synthesize the teachings of scripture, read in light of Luther's new theological insights, gave rise to a nuance of Luther's Protestantism. Christians today who follow Calvin are referred to as members of the "Reformed" or "Presbyterian" church. Their beliefs are summed up in the claims of several historical councils, but the foundational doctrines that guide what they believe can be found in John Calvin's 1536 work entitled *Institutes of the Christian Religion*.

In this massive work, which serves as a summary of the teachings he claims to have found in Christian scripture, Calvin lays out his fundamental beliefs. The work as a whole is made up of four divisions, or "books," which are organized according to the ancient Christian statement of belief, "The Apostles' Creed."

In Book I, Calvin explores the relationship between God the Creator and the world as creation. He asserts that every person has access to knowledge of God through creation but that this knowledge has been stifled by the existence of sin before God. Thus, God's written word, the Bible, is needed for specific, saving knowledge of God. In Book II, Calvin continues his exploration of God by focusing on God's character as Redeemer. He considers "original sin" to be the revolt of Adam and Eve in the Garden of Eden which enslaved all of humanity to ignorance and deprived them of free will. With their faculties so damaged, humans have no choice but to seek redemption apart from themselves, in Jesus. In Book III, Calvin shows how humans can be joined with Jesus by the power of the Holy Spirit. According to Calvin, faith, or belief in the saving power of God, leads to justification, which is the event of being made righteous before God. This justification can only occur when an individual trusts God for salvation, not by attempting to earn righteousness by good works. Calvin maintains that God is too perfect to be impressed with our petty attempts at holiness, and the Christian must assume that salvation is made possible, not by a person's choice to follow God, but by God's choice to redeem that person. Finally, in Book IV, Calvin explores the church, which is the particular means by which the Holy Spirit calls and equips Christian believers. The church should be united, "as the mother of all the godly," yet according to Calvin the church of Rome, the Catholic Church, is not the true one. The church that is true is one made up of sincere Christian believers whose hearts have been changed by the Holy Spirit.

73

As the Protestant Reformation increasingly progressed, a number of Protestant denominations arose in France, Switzerland, and the Netherlands that were united in their shared love for the teachings of John Calvin. These groups were eventually associated with national churches in which ecclesial and state government were juxtaposed. A number of these institutions eventually expanded or split into a variety of denominations, and today there are over 700 Christian groups worldwide that associate themselves with Calvin. They are referred to as "Reformed" or "Presbyterian" churches.

Fundamental to these statements are a handful of beliefs that separate reformers from other Christians. Among them are the following: First, reformed Christians maintain that God's gracious act of salvation always precedes faith. That is, because humans want to be careful to preserve God's glory and freedom, reformed Christians believe that God chooses the saved, not vice versa. To assert otherwise, according to these believers, is to elevate the human to a level equal to God, since the human's work is able to persuade God. This belief allows reformed Christians to carry into their worship the Catholic practice of infant baptism, according to which the infant is considered included in the Christian community before they make a decision themselves to join it. Second, reformed Christians believe in the "priesthood of all believers," a teaching that served as a rallying cry during the earliest periods of the

Protestant Reformation. According to this teaching, there are no Christians who have special access to God. Because all believers are able to commune with God only through the mediation of Jesus, and since Christian scripture teaches that Jesus is the only "High Priest," reformed Christians assert that no one believer has a special claim of access to God. Thus, all believers are priests, and all believers should be considered equal. Third, related to their belief in the priesthood of all believers, reformed Christians maintain that leadership of the church should be shared by a plurality of church members and should not be placed in the hands of a solitary bishop or pope. They typically follow either a "Presbyterian polity," in which levels of assemblies of elders govern the church, or a "Congregationalist polity," in which local churches maintain governmental autonomy.

It was a number of Reformed churches, especially those rooted in a Calvinistic understanding of the relationship between civic rule and ecclesial rule that together came to the Americas during the religious persecution of the 16th and 17th centuries in Europe. This Calvinistic worldview, mediated by American theologians like Jonathan Edwards, eventually gave a religious fervor to the America Revolution that cannot be ignored by modern historians.

Today there are two large Presbyterian denominations in America, the Presbyterian Church, USA, and its conservative counterpart, the Presbyterian Church in America. Between these two denominations are approximately three million members. Other reformed denominations include the Reformed Church in America and the Christian Reformed Church, both of which have roots in Dutch Calvinism.

Hollywood represents the decadence of celebrities: wealthy, politically liberal, and is disassociated from the morals of mainstream America.

. . . .

DAY TWENTY SEVEN :: THURSDAY
OCTOBER 9, 2008
"Never give up and sit down and grieve. Find another way."
— Richard Nixon, 37th American President, (1913-1994)

Yom Kippur, like Rosh Hashanah is not fixed on the same date every year, but it moves with the Jewish calendar, so next year Yom Kippur is on October 28. On Yom Kippur, Jews dress in a Kittel, a clean, white penitential robe reminiscent of burial shrouds. Rabbi Pager explained the symbolism of this dress stating that "Jews dressed this way so they step beyond life itself to atone and return, that they may live and not die, that they may be worthy of the love that creates and sustains them."

The meanings of love, peace, and care are to be found in all religions and beliefs, it is just a matter of finding a way to see them in others then share them. Although love is a pleasant word and state of being, some people might prefer to focus on the meaning of hatred and violence which is easier to find.

. . . .

DAY TWENTY EIGHT :: FRIDAY
OCTOBER 10, 2008
THIS HIGH HOLIDAY FOR JEWS IS ONE OF REPENTANCE AND ATONEMENT.
"Hollywood is a place where they'll pay you a thousand dollars for a kiss and fifty cents for your soul."
— Marilyn Monroe, American Actress, (1926-1962)

Americans often attend movies on Friday and Saturday nights, and so I did too. I attended the movie "Body of Lies" with a physician friend who lived in my building and was originally from Afghanistan. Entertainment is a major business in the United States. Americans get most of their entertainment from either television or movies. Most homes own at least one television. Television shows on public channels, like NBC or CBS, can be broken up loosely into daytime and nighttime broadcasting. Daytime shows are usually either talk shows or soap operas. Nighttime shows are sitcoms, one-hour dramas, and late-night talk shows. In addition to the public channels, many Americans purchase large packages of additional channels, many of which are devoted to a certain genre, audience, or theme. There are exclusive television channels for comedy, sports, news, and do-it-yourself home improvement.

Americans also enjoy movies. Popular American cinema focuses on comedy, action, and romance. During the summer, movie studios will try to release "blockbuster" movies with large budgets, filled with action, violence, and some kind of love story in order to draw huge crowds. In the summer of 2008, "The Dark Knight" featured guns, explosions, murders, and a romantic rivalry; and, despite increasing economic pressures, it easily broke records for opening weekend profits, and theaters remained sold-out for weeks after its premiere.

While Americans love movies, many are critical of the violence and sex depicted on the big screen. The symbol of this problem is Hollywood, a section of Los Angeles, California, where most of the major movie studios have been located since the 1910s. Hollywood represents the decadence of celebrities: wealthy, politically liberal, and is disassociated from the morals of mainstream America. It also represents the exploitation of human appetites for money. Conservative politicians attack Hollywood for contributing to the corruption of public morality. But Hollywood also symbolizes the glamour and excitement of fame; and even Americans politically offended by Hollywood love to discuss news and gossip about celebrities' lives, an interest to which several television channels are dedicated.

International films generally do not receive popular attention from Americans, except perhaps on college campuses, partially because foreign films are only released in major cities like New York and Chicago. Certain international films can enjoy a broad underground popularity, like kung-fu movies, but only a handful of films, with translated soundtracks, do well with American audiences. On the other hand, international television shows adapted for American audiences can be very popular. "The Office" was originally a British comedy, but has become a hit in America; though only after being re-filmed with American actors.

. .. .

DAY TWENTY NINE :: SATURDAY
OCTOBER 11, 2008
"If you can dream it, you can do it. Always remember that this whole thing was started with a dream and a mouse."

— Walt Disney, American Film Producer, (1901-1966)

My neighbors Anton and Nadia, whom I met at the lounge of my residence, enjoy many things, and they enjoy having intellectual conversations the most. They kindly introduced me to our neighborhood, showed me places for Jazz and Pops, the movie theater, and nice restaurants. Anton's favorite topic is American history, while Nadia always likes to talk about politics and she knows it well because she is originally from Russia. It seems to me that the black mark of American history and culture is violence. When Columbus arrived, his first impression was that with 50 people he could overtake the Native American's land and have them do whatever he wants. The Natives were massacred when the Europeans arrived to America. Slavery is another issue America experienced and overcame, but slavery was not an American phenomenon like the massacre of the Natives.

. .. .

DAY THIRTY :: SUNDAY
OCTOBER 12, 2008
"Time is what we want most, but what we use worst."
> — William Penn, American founder of Pennsylvania, (1644-1718)

A s we attend the celebration of Jewish Sabbath at the end of first week of our arrival to the U.S., I realize today that Christian too celebrate Sabbath on Sunday. Unlike Jews, Christians do chores, go shopping, and participate in other activities besides worshiping at the churches on Sunday. However, Sunday is different than the rest of the week; people tend to wake up a bit late, and many would go to church in the morning. After noon, they usually stay at home with their families and get themselves or their children ready for school and the week ahead.

. .. .

DAY THIRTY ONE :: MONDAY
OCTOBER 13, 2008
"Gym membership today fills the same role as church membership did more than a century ago. It is a testament of character."
> — Ronald Dworkin, American Philosopher, (1931-)

I had a brief meeting this morning with Bill to go over my schedule for the upcoming two months at Loyola University. Once the schedule was set, I could see what time might be free to join a gym for exercise. In Saudi Arabia, this practice is not common, but in the U.S. and Canada it is one of the most popular forms of physical exercise. Also, part of my two-month regime would be to find a late-night café where I could write. I enjoyed the company of the student community that gathered at the café I frequented near Northwestern University.

I also spent time this day on the web with my ICAP friends. Before departing from Philadelphia, I formed a web-based dialogue forum for the ICAP group where we would share interfaith and intra-faith dialogues based on what we were experiencing. One of the longest intra-faith dialogues we had was initiated today by Serge. This excerpt is taken from a conversation between Serge and Michael about women priests in the Catholic Church.

Dear Serge,

The issue of women's ordination has been a long-drawn issue within the Catholic Church. It must be important to note that the question is never about sociological or functional perspectives or gender issues but a theological one. This is unlike the discussion on priestly celibacy which is admittedly a disciplinary norm which theoretically can be changed in the future. I'm attaching an article which my friend wrote in a local journal recently — it explains the Church's official position about women's ordination. I personally have no doubt that many women are more than able to carry out pastoral duties (and they are doing so) with the thoughtful authenticity and sensitivity which they bring to ministry. But the issue of holy orders (priesthood) is an ontological one, not a functional one. I write this aware of the possibility that I'll be accused of being a male-chauvinist pig. But I'd rather be theologically correct than politically correct. Unfortunately, contemporary society often places greater emphasis on political correctness rather than theological truths.

I would agree that our conscience should be the ultimate measure of conduct. It is the internal criteria of morality according to Catholic moral theology. But, it is also true that the internal criteria, which is our conscience, needs to be informed by the external criteria, which includes revelation, the church's magisterium, personal experience and context. Therefore, applying the 'conscience' argument is never a license to do whatever you want without any external accountability. True conscience needs to be exercised in communion with the larger community (in the case of Christians, it is the church).

Last Sunday's gospel reading was informative. It was the parable of the king and the wedding feast. The king does appear to look like a capricious despot that punishes people for not having accepted his hospitality and for not conforming to the proper dress code. I believe that the parable is actually a profound commentary on the meaning of salvific inclusivity. God's invitation is universal and inclusive. But it is both time limited as well as form limited. There is a time for everyone to respond to the invitation, but not always. Death closes the door on that invitation. The second portion of the parable highlights the real meaning of inclusiveness. Inclusiveness isn't about "everything works." Some things "don't work" — selfishness, self-centeredness, hatred, bigotry, etc. We are invited to join a larger polity with a single purpose — it is the king's son's wedding feast. The feast is not about us but about God. I can't dictate terms in order to change elements of the feast — the purpose of celebration, the menu, the decorations, dress code, manner of celebration, just to suit me. Inclusiveness is not a license for individuals to take their individuality to an extreme. There is always the dimension of the "other" and of "God." What are we prepared to change in ourselves for others and for God and not vice versa? For the individualistic thinker, the parable is utter nonsense and utterly "undemocratic." For those who have the community at heart, it is a reminder that life is

78

not just about "me" but always about "others" and about "God."

I will continue to treat with great respect (as I do all other religious traditions) churches that ordain women and women who have chosen ordination (both within the Catholic Church — yes there are some; and outside). But respect does not equal theological agreement. There can be theological agreement on some points but we would have to accept the possibility of disagreement on many other points. The whole point of dialogue is that we can accept persons who hold different views from us and afford them deep respect without having to change them according to our image and likeness.

I would also not want to comment about how other religions should treat this same issue. I think that the best theological arguments need to come from experts from within these religions rather than from an outsider.

Regards,

Michael

Hi Michael,

Now we will engage in an intra-dialogue. Interesting; your reaction about women priests in the Catholic Church. For our Muslims friends it would be nice if you would spell-out more clearly some of the terms you use like "the issue of holy orders (priesthood) is an ontological one, not a functional one." It's a heavy sentence. Do you mean that priesthood depends essentially on the male sex?

Your friend's article is enlightening except that he does not take into consideration the history of the female ministerial participation in the Christian communities. Some very interesting works have been done on the question. I think of the academic work done by a Jesuit Maltese, Fr. Farrugia, Professor at the Pontifical Institute of Oriental Studies, Italy. I had the joy of listening to him explain that. It was most enlightening.

The real issue according to your friend will be to hold to the fact that a priest is "Persona Christi" (Christ in person? person of Christ?). This is for me where the whole discussion would be. What do we mean by Persona Christi? Do we mean he is Christ in person? Do we mean he represents Christ? Is a Catholic priest a "persona Christi?" "persona Christi" is a heavy statement that poses even some Christological questions. Some prefer "alter Christi" (Arupe). Others propose to view the priest as "instrumentum Christi." If any Catholic priest is "persona Christi" then I think many people will never believe in Christ. Now if he is only "persona Christi" when he consecrates the bread and wine, then later what is he? You know very well where this theological expression comes from and from which theological school. Indeed there are differing theological schools in our church even if we give the impression to people that we are united in dogmatic questions. Any dogmatic statement is a problematic statement in discussion. And "ijtihad" is never closed for us.

Your friend ends his article by saying: "Some continue to say, 'Had Jesus been alive at this moment, He would have done it differently.' Well, He is alive now. And He is acting in and through his church." Is your friend serious in saying this? I would rather say with humility, Jesus is alive and he is acting in and through some members of his church. If you live in a perfect community you can say that. I have seen so much evil. I have heard so much evil. I have read about so much evil in the history of the Catholic Church that I will not even for one second say a sentence like that. Let's be real here. Unless he means the Church of Christ is not an actual community of men and women with bones and flesh. But he means the mystical body of Christ. Let's keep this definition of the Church of Christ in seminaries and books. The Church of Christ is the community of men and women with bones and flesh, the community of great sinners who are struggling every day to fight evil inside themselves and in the society.

So an important question for you will be to think of what you mean by "the church" with capital C, the Catholic Church, the large community. Does a large community exist? Do you mean the Vatican? Or do you mean all the particular small Catholic communities? Now how are those small Catholic communities "united" to form the Catholic Church? How much of the teachings of the church are actually based on a real participation of the small Catholic communities in Malaysia? Are they only receptive or are they really participating in forming the church's teaching? Or is the teaching of what you call the large community the work of theologians, bishops, and the pope, who live every day in their palace and drink and feast while the poor Catholic Lazarus is at the door! This is not bla bla bla. I told my bishop in Rwanda while he visited our parish of Kimisagara, a poor area in Kigali that he is scandalizing his Christians by coming with a land cruiser and a driver to visit them. He replied they are the ones who want me to live like this. I left the meeting. Your reading of the gospel of Sunday was beautiful. That's the beauty of the church. I would never have thought about this without your sharing. Anyway, thank you.

A very enlightening book would be *Models of the Church* by Avery Dulles. The Lunko Institute in South Africa, a Catholic institute for social justice training, also developed an understanding of the Catholic Church as a communion of communities, based on the African theology of the church as family of God, with serious implications for the actual form of governance of a parish, a diocese, and the whole church. Moreover and this is the real interesting thing how the actual community, local, particular, as small as possible could influence the teachings of the church.

By making the question theological you are giving hope that one day another theological, the people-driven school will win. Inshaa allah! Sorry for being long. I get excited with this intra-dialogue! I have to go to a seminar now. Ciao.

Serge

. . . .

DAY THIRTY TWO :: TUESDAY
OCTOBER 14, 2008
"Only if you have been in the deepest valley, can you ever know how magnificent it is to be on the highest mountain."

— Richard Nixon, 37th American President, (1913-1994)

Today is Sukkot, and it is noticeable in all Jews homes and neighborhoods by the decorative fruits and trees around their homes. If you know a Jews family, you will be most likely invited to their home to share a meal or snack with them. Sukkot is a biblical pilgrimage festival that occurs in autumn on the full moon, the 15th day of the month of Tishrei, which falls in late September to late October in the secular calendar. Sukkot is a seven day holiday, with the first day celebrated as a full festival with special prayer services and holiday meals. The remaining days are known as Chol HaMoed "festival weekdays." Sukkot is one of the three major holidays known collectively as the Shalosh Regalim, i.e., three pilgrim festivals, when Jews from all over Eretz Yisrael, and even surrounding countries, traveled to celebrate in the Temple in Jerusalem.

The word Sukkot is the plural of the Hebrew word sukkah, meaning booth or hut. The sukkah is reminiscent of the type of temporary shelters in which the ancient Israelites dwelt during their 40 years of wandering in the desert after the Exodus from Mitzrayim. Its roof, decorated with the leafy stalks and fruits of the field's harvest make each family's sukkah like the harvest huts built in the fields during the fall harvest. The holiday has mystical significance as well, as does the entire cycle of Jewish holidays. Throughout the holiday, festive meals are eaten in the sukkah, and some families sleep there.

Not only Jewish festivals are celebrated and noticed in America, but if you live there you will notice, depending on your neighborhood, many religious, nationalist, and cultural events celebrated all over the States. This one for Jews commemorates a time when they were lost and disoriented in the desert; that experience means they now know better how to be grateful for their homes and in turn want to be hospitable.

. . . .

DAY THIRTY THREE :: WEDNESDAY
OCTOBER 15, 2008
"Never go out to meet trouble. If you just sit still, nine cases out of ten, someone will intercept it before it reaches you."

— Calvin Coolidge, 30th American President, (1872-1933)

. . ..

DAY THIRTY FOUR :: THURSDAY
OCTOBER 16, 2008

"Someday, following the example of the United States of America, there will be a United States of Europe."

— George Washington, 1st American President, (1732-1799)

. . ..

DAY THIRTY FIVE :: FRIDAY
OCTOBER 17, 2008

"If a nation expects to be ignorant and free, it expects what never was and never will be. ...When the press is free and every man can read, all is safe."

— Thomas Jefferson, 3rd American President, (1743-1826)

. . ..

DAY THIRTY SIX :: SATURDAY
OCTOBER 18, 2008

"If you're going to America, bring your own food."

— Fran Lebowitz, American Writer, (1950-)

Lately, I tend to have Saturdays off and I try to relax. A friend of mine, who is studying for his M.A. degree in Ohio, came to visit me. I took him to a Thai restaurant for lunch and then we went to Michigan Avenue in downtown Chicago despite several Chicagoans having told me that downtown Chicago was not that much fun. In general, major American cities are no longer centered downtown as they used to be. Now differing parts of the city take on differing personalities. For example, the malls are in one place, young people's clubs are in another, fine restaurants are elsewhere and the museums are in yet another part of the city. It has become more convenient for the majority of Americans to live in the suburbs of cities where neighborhoods are generally safer, more modern, and necessary services are all nearby.

A Russian friend who used to study in Saudi Arabia knew I was in Chicago so he also came to visit me. His story is not so different from many Muslim immigrants who come to the States either by the lottery or marriage. In his case, there is a combination of the two because his wife came to the States by lottery and he came after he married her, but still had not gotten his green card due to homeland security restrictions. Everyone who has experienced difficulty in travel or immigration to the U.S. agrees that the homeland security issue is exaggerated, but I still don't think anyone has the right to blame Americans for taking security issues very seriously.

83

. . ..

DAY THIRTY SEVEN :: SUNDAY
OCTOBER 19, 2008
"Repetition does not transform a lie into a truth."
— Franklin Roosevelt, 32nd American President, (1882-1945)

I t is the holy day of atonement in Sister Clara Mosque, commemorating the 13th anniversary of the Million Man March. Today, Louis Farrakhan will rededicate the mosque, giving it a new name—Maryam "a new beginning for the Nation of Islam."
But before describing this day and its significance, it is important to understand the background of the day's event. Louis Farrakhan, Nation of Islam (NOI) leader, called for The Million Man March in Washington D.C. on October 16, 1995. The March was described as a call to Black men to take charge and rebuild their communities by showing more respect for themselves and devotion to their families. It is estimated that over two million attended the March. Not long after that, on February 25, 2000, Louis Farrakhan announced an end to the 25-year-long rift between the Nation of Islam and the Moslem American Society headed by Wallace Deen Mohammed who passed away just few days before my arrival to America. The groups had split in 1975 following the death of Elijah Muhammad, the founder of the Nation of Islam.

The ceremony began with a recitation of the Quran by Ahmed Tijani, followed by the three calls to prayer starting with the Shofar of Jews, then the Bell of Christians, then the Athan of the Muslims. After the calls to prayer, three prayers were offered: the first was by a Jewish rabbi; then a Christian reverend; then a Muslim imam. After these three prayers the Minister Louis Farrakhan named this Mosque after the mother of Jesus to let this dominant Christian country know and understand that every Muslim believes in Jesus.

   This mosque was built on 1950 as a Catholic Church, and when Elijah Muhammad entered it, he decided to buy it and have it as a mosque, which he did in 1972. Farrakhan bought the mosque from Warithuddn (Wallace) Muhammad, the son of Elijah Muhammad with funds from NOI members and rebuilt it in 1988. He then he received funds from Turkey to decorate and furnish it.

   Minister Ishmael Muhammad gave a speech about the history of this mosque. Following this speech, a song by Franz Schubert was dedicated to Maryam. Farrakhan gave the sermon of dedication followed by a prayer of dedication.

   Farrakhan thanked God for many things in the beginning of his speech, first for guiding him and his teacher Elijah Muhammad on the right path. Second for sending messengers to people, especially to the Prophets: Moses with the Torah, Jesus with the Gospel, and Muhammad with the Quran, peace be upon them all. Then third for having Fard, the person who is said by NOI to represent God on Earth, to send Elijah as a messenger to us (here Farrakhan states that Elijah was sent as a messenger). Then fourth he thanks God for listening to the music in the mosque for the first time in twenty years. After the lengthy speech that lasted for about ninety minutes, Farrakhan made a prayer and recited Quran. He read al-Fatiha, the opening chapter of the Quran. He learned how to read it from Malek Shabbaz (Malcolm X) as I was told later. The ceremony concluded with more music.

   Farrakhan's guests were invited to Salam Restaurant, an establishment which was funded by Kaddafi of Libya with about five million dollars. Farrakhan went to greet people, and I had two short conversations with him, one at the mosque where I thanked him for his speech and he told me that I should consider Maryam Mosque as my mosque

I discussed the new change within NOI with
Farakhan during a dinner in Chicago.

and that I can come to pray anytime; then we hugged each other. I didn't realize at the time the historical shift in NOI this event represented. Later I learned that before this event, non-Black Muslims were not allowed to enter NOI's mosques. Farrakhan's change was huge; he turned the NOI into a universal organization. In other words, NOI had been in a self-improving stage for decades and now they were ready to involve themselves with the global community of Muslims. After dinner I had another short conversation with Farrakhan and as he had to go to greet other guests. I asked him if it is possible to meet with him later on for ten to fifteen minutes. He then invited me to have dinner with him and asked his minister Ahmed Tijani to make the arrangements with me. I talked with Tijani for an hour about the past and present situation of NOI. We decide to meet in few days to continue our discussion.

At our table were also a few Palestinian Muslim leaders, Malek Shabbaz a radical Muslim, as he described himself, and some NOI members. The discussion was about the Israeli- Arab conflict. Apparently my views were different than the rest of the people at the table. The discussion turned to the Shi'i Lebanese Hezbollah, and I was not in favor of its leader Hassan Nasrallah which didn't please others. I was surprised by how media can influence people's mind. When I was in Beirut in 2006 and 2008, I saw how non-southern Lebanese are unhappy with Hezbollah. The conversation shifted to the dialogue among civilizations and the interfaith dialogue among the Abrahamic religions in particular. NOI members think such dialogue would only be possible if Obama were to win the election.

. . ..

DAY THIRTY EIGHT :: MONDAY
OCTOBER 20, 2008
"There are no accidents in my philosophy. Every effect must have its cause. The past is the cause of the present, and the present will be the cause of the future. All these are links in the endless chain, stretching from the finite to the infinite."
 — Abraham Lincoln, 16th American President, (1809-1865)

In Saudi Arabia, we have a proverb that says "a chance is better than thousand appointments." Today Professor William popped into the Connection Café inside the Cohan Library unexpectedly and a good conversation ensured. The discussion was mainly about Catholic hierarchy. The Catholic Church is run by deacons introduced into the Catholic Church by the second Vatican Conference in 1962. Deacons serve two of the seven sacraments which are the baptism and Holy Orders or Communion. The remaining five sacraments are done by priests only, and they are Confirmation, Eucharist, Penance, Anointing of the Sick, and Matrimony. In addition to the deacons, laypersons can do many of the church's daily responsibilities other than the sacraments.

Deacons work for priests who run a parish, a neighborhood of Catholics. Priests take three major vows: one is for poverty which means they cannot own property, the second is for chastity which means they cannot get married, and third is for obedience which means they have to obey their higher religious leaders. Priests in large regions are led by a bishop who leads the diocese, and if the diocese is very large then more than one bishop will serve. The next largest region is an archdiocese where an archbishop will be in charge. Some bishops are appointed by the pope to be cardinals, and there are about one hundred forty cardinals in the world. Some of those cardinals are based in the Vatican. In very rare cases the pope may appoint priests to be cardinals. The cardinals elect the pope who is at the top of the hierarchy and runs the whole Catholic institution.

Another system in Catholicism is the one of religious orders which usually run either schools or hospitals. One of the religious orders, for example, is the Jesuit order which runs Loyola University. In the religious orders there are priests who are led by a priest leader who reports to the pope directly, not to the bishop, in the same geographical region. In this religious order there are usually many sisters, nuns, and laypeople who serve in the church. There are hundreds of religious orders other than Jesuits, like Benedictines and Franciscans.

Learning about Catholic beliefs or other Christian doctrines encouraged me to reread many books on religions that were not written by the authority or followers of that religion. I was telling Professor William how sad it was to find books introducing

The pope is at the top of the hierarchy and runs the whole Catholic institution. Catholics recognize the Pope as a successor to Saint Peter, who according to Catholic teaching, was one of Jesus' first disciples and the first pope of the Catholic church.

religions that do not represent the religion, but rather represent the interpretation of a minor group within a religion. In those books, authors tend to try to discredit the religion and therefore end up fostering hatred and disrespect for their followers. The approach I am attempting to adopt is to show the greatness of the differing religions, knowing that they share the same principles, yet have different ways, interpretations, and practices by which to apply those principals. Therefore, people should respect religions despite the differences in practice among them.

That afternoon Professor Akhtarul Wasey presented a lecture on Indian Muslim intellectuals that covered most of the Indian scholars, from orthodox to secular, as well as the dialogue that is going on between Muslims and Hindus. At the end of the lecture several questions, views, and comments were raised. The most enlightened comment focused on the dialogue between the west and east written down by Muslim scholars who wrote their works during confrontation of the colonial era. Thus, the writings of Sayyed Qutb, Maududi and other Muslim leaders should be regarded in the context of that confrontation. Professor Wasey commented that we should focus on the context not the text. It is a necessity to rewrite an Islamic perspective today of the dialogue among civilizations taking into consideration the global change in the world and the need for peace, common interest, and shared values. We all agreed there is a need to rewrite a Muslim view of American culture to correct the views presented by Sayyed Qutb in his book about America, as well as other related books by different Arab authors.

. .. .

DAY THIRTY NINE :: TUESDAY
OCTOBER 21, 2008

"America is not like a blanket — one piece of unbroken cloth, the same color, the same texture, the same size. America is more like a quilt — many patches, many pieces, many colors, and many sizes, all woven and held together by a common thread."

— Jesse Jackson, American Activist, (1941-)

America is a very big country, and American culture is the most complicated culture on this planet. Americans have disparate ways of life to the point where they have no unified way of life. They tend to standardize every measurable materialistic thing, but they do not standardize their thoughts on morality and emotion. One of my essential conclusions about American culture is that we must differentiate between the culture of the community and that of the individuals. Unlike my part of the world, where one public school represents all other schools, and one person of a city shows you almost an exact sample of the rest of people in his or her city or tribe, American individuals, schools, and cities are all unique and you cannot name one certain behavior, theology, methodology, philosophy for all Americans.

. .. .

DAY FORTY :: WEDNESDAY
OCTOBER 22, 2008
"I look forward to a future in which our country will match its military strength with our moral restraint, its wealth with our wisdom, its power with our purpose."
— John F. Kennedy, 35th American President, (1917-1963)

At noon we had a short talk and open discussion with the Theology Department at Loyola University followed by lunch with the faculty members. After brief introductions by the department's professors, I realized how different this religious department's structure is from that of an Islamic one. I talked with the head of the administrative office at the department about it and she explained to me that the theology departments usually consist of four programs: Constructive Theology, Historical Theology, Ethics, and Biblical Studies.

Constructive Theology is the re-definition of what has historically been known as systematic theology. The reason for this reevaluation stems from the idea that, in systematic theology, the theologian attempts to develop a coherent theory running through the various doctrines within the tradition. A potential problem underlying such study is that in constructing a system of theology, certain elements may be left out, or "forced" into categories in order to maintain the coherence of the overall system. Many contemporary theologians feel that the term "systematic" is no longer accurate in reference to theology, and therefore prefer the language of constructive theology.

Historical Theology is a branch of theological studies that investigates the socio-historical and cultural mechanisms that give rise to theological ideas, systems, and statements. Research and method in this field focuses on the relationship between theology and context as well as the major theological influences upon the figures and topics studied. Historical theologians are thus concerned with the historical development of theology.

Ethics is a branch of philosophy dealing with right and wrong in human behavior. Most religions have a moral component, and religious approaches to ethical questions. Religious approaches to ethics dominate secular approaches. From the point of view of theistic religions, ethics is studied as a branch of theology to the extent that ethics stems from revealed truth from divine sources. Many believe that the Golden Rule, which teaches people to "treat others as they want to be treated," is a common denominator among many major moral codes and religions.

Biblical Studies is the academic study of the Judeo-Christian Bible and related texts. For Christianity, the Bible traditionally comprises the New Testament and Old Testament, which together are sometimes called the scriptures. Judaism only recognizes the Hebrew Bible as scripture, also known as the Tanakh, an acronym for the Hebrew names of its divisions: Torah (Law), Nevi'im (Prophets) and Ketuvim (writings). Other texts often examined by biblical scholars include the Jewish apocrypha, the Jewish pseudepigrapha, the Christian apocrypha, the many varieties of ante-Nicene early Christian literature, and early Jewish literature. There are two major approaches towards Biblical Studies. The first approach studies the Bible as a human creation and is also known as biblical criticism; this approach is practiced in the secular academic world. In this approach, Biblical Studies can be considered as a sub-field of Religious Studies. The other approach is the religious study of the Bible, where it is assumed that the Bible has a divine origin. This approach is a branch of theology, and is also known as biblical interpretation or hermeneutics.

Chapter 4

"*Our Constitution was made only for a moral and religious people. It is wholly inadequate to the government of any other.*"

John Adams, 2ND AMERICAN PRESIDENT, (1735-1826)

. .. .

DAY FORTY ONE :: THURSDAY
OCTOBER 23, 2008
"Nobody can give you freedom. Nobody can give you equality or justice or anything.
If you're a man, you take it."
> — Malcolm X, American activist, (1925-1965).

Continuing my discussion with Tijani about NOI, he invited me to his home where we had a lengthy discussion about African Americans. Tijani was talking with deep emotion and a raised voice about the history of Black people when they first arrived to America. He felt that the experiences that African Americans had faced were more than sufficient to convince them to be involved with any movement that would elevate their situation from seeming more similar to an animal than a human being. It went on to the extent of a revolution that would require them to believe that God is Black or Heaven will be reserved for Black people alone and other beliefs called to by the Fard, who claims to be God in person, and later sent Elijah as a messenger of God to Black people.

Americans endeavor the situation of slaves gradually. Once, I met with the American ambassador in Riyadh and among the topics we discussed was how America overcame problems caused by slavery. His short and sweet answer was simply, law. America's social, political, and economic challenges toward slavery were solved over time with rules and laws that establish equal rights and opportunities. Today we can see how equal opportunity has led America to have an African American in its highest leadership position.

. .. .

DAY FORTY TWO :: FRIDAY
OCTOBER 24, 2008
"Today we can declare: Government is not the problem, and government is not the solution.
We, the American people, we are the solution."
> — William J. Clinton, 42nd American President, (1946-).

Seventy-nine years ago today was Black Thursday; the day that started the Great Depression. This worldwide economic collapse lasted from 1929 to 1941. Although the Depression had effects worldwide, it originated in the United States and had its most devastating effects there. Experts still do not fully understand its origins, but there are several conditions that contributed to its intensity. During the historic period called the Roaring '20s, America had experienced a boom of

◄ *Baha'i temple*

*I visited the Baha'i temple with Asif. The existence of
Baha'i and their practices show the freedom of religion
that America offers, which explain the diversity of
religions living peacefully in one nation.*

productivity and prosperity fueled by the new automobile industry. But production
increased much more quickly than wages, resulting in a supply surplus that the workers
could not afford to absorb. Indeed, a significant disparity developed between the rich
and the poor. At first, businesses tried to resolve the problem by developing installment
credit plans by which people could acquire expensive goods now, and pay for them
in small increments over time. But, when workers were forced to spend all of their
wages on essential goods, they were unable to pay the installments; credit had only
delayed the damage. The rich, on the other hand, centralized a vast amount of wealth
into few hands, which they were incapable of spending quickly enough to keep goods
circulating. There was an enormous amount of stock market speculation, often funded
by buying stocks on margin, that is, on borrowed money with the intent to pay later.
In October 1929, the stock market crashed, wiping out billions of dollars, emptying
out lending institutions and further restricting spending that was already anemic. This
wealth imbalance caused a lack of consumption, and the Great Crash of 1929, resulted
in the Great Depression.

There was vast poverty and misery during the Depression. Unemployment jumped
to 25%. Millions of homeless Americans lived as transients and collected in large
communities where they made huts from cheap, available materials; these towns
were named "Hoovervilles" named after the current President Herbert Hoover, who
proved incapable of orchestrating an economic recovery. In addition to these disasters,
severe drought, combined with poor agricultural techniques used in the Southern
Plains section of America, such as Kansas, became known as the "Dust Bowl." After
the farmers had exhausted the soil, crops and grass refused to grow; the lifeless soil
was picked up by the powerful plains winds, which created huge dust storms capable
of blocking out the sun. While Roosevelt's New Deal tried to promote growth and
recovery, and successfully improved unemployment, America would not come out of
the Great Depression until it entered World War II.

Currently, the world is suffering the worst economic downturn since the Great Depression. The so-called "Great Recession" has its origins in the housing market. American banks had been lending huge sums of money for mortgages. The reasoning was that these loans would eventually be paid; they were constructed as an intricate financial system, allowing them to trade loans and risk money on the basis of eventual repayment. The financial system convinced bankers that they could make money if they continued to lend it, and so they made a number of bad loans. The continuing deregulation of the housing market, however, allowed for the deceptive repackaging of loans. This dynamic, combined with meager growth in American wages, eventually resulted in widespread defaulting, which in turn caused the system of mortgage sales and futures betting to collapse. This collapse mirrors the Depression insofar as it originated from a combination of diminished purchasing power among the lower classes combined with stock market speculation that was unfounded in real production.

After Friday prayer at the Bosnian mosque, I went with Asif to the Baha'i temple. On our way we talked about Baha'i faith which I know nothing about other than they believe in a modern prophet and they originated somewhere in India. Asif told me that they were actually in Iran and he also does not know much about them but he has visited their temple where we were heading. When we arrived, we found other people visiting the temple as it had become more like a tourist site, where people visit its marvelous garden and even have their wedding receptions. Like all Baha'i houses of worship, the temple in Wilmette is circular in shape, has nine sides, and is surrounded by exquisite gardens and fountains. There were two Iranians at the door: Asher, who works there and seemed to be knowledgeable and speak Arabic, Persian, and English fluently, and an elderly Iranian woman who seemed enthusiastic but did not really know much of the details about the Baha'i faith.

The principle of the oneness of humankind is the axis for which all the teachings of Baha'i faith revolve. Baha'u'llah announced in 1863 that he is God's messenger for this age. His teachings and sacred writings are the basis of the Baha'i Faith. There are seven major Baha'i shrines around the world, including the one I visited in Chicago, IL. Most Baha'i religious practices are private, such as praying and accepting donations. The International Baha'i Fund, administered by the Universal House of Justice, supports the growth and development of the faith throughout the world. The Fund also helps maintain the faith's sacred shrines and other endowments at the Baha'i World Center in Haifa, Israel. The existence of Baha'i and their practices show the freedom of religion that America offers, which explain the diversity of religions living peacefully in one nation.

DAY FORTY THREE :: SATURDAY
OCTOBER 25, 2008

"When the government fears the people, it is liberty. When the people fear the government, it is tyranny."

— Thomas Paine, American Writer, (1737-1809)

It is appropriate to shed a light on religion with some statistics. Among Americans, over 85% are affiliated with religions. These affiliations are as follows; Protestant 51.3%, Roman Catholic 23.9%, Mormon 1.7%, other Christian 1.6%, Jewish 1.7%, Buddhist 0.7%, Muslim 0.6%, other or unspecified 2.5%, unaffiliated 12.1%, none 4% (2007 est.)

Diversity is not in religions only, but in ethnical background as well. We find the American background varies as follows; White 79.96%, Black 12.85%, Asian 4.43%, Amerindian and Alaska native 0.97%, native Hawaiian and other Pacific islander 0.18%, two or more races 1.61%, about 15.1% of the total U.S. population is Hispanic (July 2007 estimate). This varied ethnical background led to the multi languages existed in the U.S.; these languages are; English 82.1%, Spanish 10.7%, other Indo-European 3.8%, Asian and Pacific island 2.7%, other 0.7% (2000 census).

There are other related figures such as the age structure, age median, and other population statistics. Although America is the third most highly populated country in the world with 307,212,123 (July 2009 est.), the growth rate is comparatively low, 0.977% (2009 est.) positioning America 130th in the world, with a birth rate of 13.83 births/1,000 population (2009 est.) positioning itself 154th in the world. The sex ratio is .97 male/female (2009 est.)

DAY FORTY FOUR :: SUNDAY
OCTOBER 26, 2008

"Right is right, even if everyone is against it, and wrong is wrong, even if everyone is for it."

— William Penn, American founder of Pennsylvania, (1644-1718)

Last week, I arranged with Professor Aana to go with her to her Lutheran Church at Addison Station. She picked me up at ten in the morning with her partner Alison, and their son Benjamin. It was a sunny day, and we arrived about 5 minutes before the service began. We met a few members of the church and then we took our places in the pews somewhere in the middle of the sanctuary. The Lutheran church service seems much simpler than its Catholic counterpart. There are no paintings on the walls or windows as Luther taught that people should learn by themselves and should read the Holy Scriptures to understand the teachings of Jesus instead of relying on the translation of the priests, which happened in the Catholic Church. Perhaps the tremendous amount of paintings in the Catholic Churches was to help interpret the priest's messages. This Lutheran service included several readings from the book of Psalms and the Christian testament. Private prayers were done individually every now and then, with the organ providing much music. Towards the end, the wine and bread were served and practitioners participated in communion. In this liturgical remembrance of the last supper Jesus shared with his disciples, everyone who so chooses gets in line to eat bread and drink wine. They understood that I do not drink wine or practice Christianity and they respectfully accepted that I could only observe their practice. The service ended with each person greeting others by saying, "Peace be with you." The other person would then respond, "And with you."

After the service and in a nice sunny day we walked in the neighborhood and had lunch. After we finished, the waiter brought the menu for coffee. I noticed an item on the coffee menu called "bottomless coffee," and I asked Aana what kind of coffee is this? She said it is just an American coffee but they keep refilling it for you with the same price. Even though their coffee is bottomless, there is a crucial problem in America when it comes to food and drink; those who don't watch their weight are waiting for a disaster to happen. Overweight persons, and obesity are common phenomena among Americans of all ages, races and genders, especially when you see "bottomless" on restaurant menus. It needs to be addressed on a large scale.

. . ..

DAY FORTY FIVE :: MONDAY
OCTOBER 27, 2008
"Those who do not learn from the mistakes of history are doomed to repeat them."
— George Santayana, American philosopher, (1863-1952)

A fter my talk with the faculty members of the Theology Department last Wednesday, the conversation continued with several faculty members, through email and over coffee or food. One of the most interesting conversations, and pardon me while I adopt the American style of exaggerating, but I had a really interesting discussion with Dennis Martin, an associate Professor of Historical Theology who expressed his appreciation of my thoughts in the talk presented at lunch. He asked about public worship for Christians in Saudi Arabia. As he explained later, he raised the question largely because he had heard the head of the Theology Department express the view that Christianity could be openly practiced in Saudi Arabia. Martin fully understands how it would be impossible to go from a highly restricted private practice to permitting public Christian worship overnight. He was under the impression that open Christian worship was still not possible and wanted some clarification. I told him his sense of this reality was accurate.

In my luncheon talk, Martin noted that I was interested in learning more about Christianity and that I had mentioned the Quakers. So he explained that they come from one end of the Christian spectrum that was minimalist in worship, structure, and institution. At the other end of the spectrum are the Eastern Orthodox and Catholics, who traditionally had the highest level of structure, canon law, liturgy, etc. He went on to give me a helpful overview from his perspective of this broad spectrum of Christianity.

As a historian, Martin conveyed his understanding that Catholics underwent an overnight transformation in their liturgy about forty years ago. Under the influence of a modern/ post-modern antipathy toward structure and rules, the traditional liturgy was changed overnight. It led to a serious alienation or anomie among Catholics, many of whom left the church. Pope Benedict gave a programmatic talk in December 2005 in which he enunciated a theme he had first announced as Cardinal Ratzinger in 1985: the overnight transformation, the rupture in continuity had serious negative effects and must be addressed. His writings, in-fact his entire pontificate in some ways, have focused on overcoming what he sees as a rupture that need not have taken place, but did.

The traditional Catholic liturgy was centered on ancient religious concepts of sacrifice and atonement which arose out of Judaism. The radical changes of forty years ago among Catholics (some of which were actually not authorized but took place anyway) in many respects drastically modified the atonement elements and moved Catholic liturgy much closer to the Enlightenment/Protestant cerebral, propositional approach. Attentively, Martin lent me a DVD of the traditional liturgy which would give me an idea of the way Western Christians worshiped for 1300 years (from about 600-1950, with roots that stretched much further back into time). He also offered to take me to see one of these liturgies in action, but most commonly they are held on Sundays, at noon; less elaborate versions are available on Wednesday nights and Saturday mornings. Unfortunately, my schedule was already full for the upcoming weekends.

DAY FORTY SIX :: TUESDAY
OCTOBER 28, 2008
"Our Constitution was made only for a moral and religious people. It is wholly inadequate to the government of any other."

— John Adams, 2nd American President, (1735-1826)

I was very taken by my conversations with Martin and we continued to exchange ideas. He explained to me that one may divide the history of the Christian Church into three major periods:

I. The origins and establishment of the basic structures of the church, accompanied by working out the controversial theological matters surrounding the nature and mission of Jesus Christ, sometimes called the Apostolic and Patristic Period, or the period of the Church Fathers (up to 600 CE).

II. The development of Christendom, of a Christian culture in Europe (600-1500 CE).

III. The breakdown of that Christian culture, which occurred simultaneously with the expansion of Christianity around the world in the wake of European colonization (1500 CE onward). Note that this last phase is not the breakdown of the church or of Christianity but the deChristianizing of western European culture.

The church remained strong but, in many ways, has been returned to the situation of the first few centuries in which to be Christian was to oppose many of the assumptions and practices of the mainstream culture. This was not true in the middle period, even though, by no means were they all living up to Christian ideals. The culture of that period, however, did take for granted that nearly all members of society were baptized Christians and were obligated by their baptism to live according to Christianity. The imperfect adherence to those obligations does not imply that their character was not Christian, but that they were most observant of their cultural interpretations. The situation since the "Enlightenment" of the 1700s and following centuries has been different. The "movers and shakers," began with a few and grew to include nearly all of them, becoming moderately then radically anti-Christian or post-Christian. This was true of most intellectual and artistic elites in Europe by the 1800s and it was recognizable in North America and Western Europe by the mid-1900s.

The modern secular movement now competes with major faith traditions around the globe. However, in my opinion, there is a crucial different between the origin and development of secularism in France and that of America. While the French Revolution was formed to eliminate religion and religious people from the public life, the call for secularity and liberty in America was to protect the freedom of religions and human rights. Secularism was rejected by religious leaders and the mainstream citizens in the Muslim World, because what has been introduced to them is the French brand of secularism. This rejection of "French Secularism" was applied as the American call for liberty. Had American liberty called for human rights, or if it had been properly introduced, it would not have been confused with "French Secularism" and thereby refused by the majority; instead it would be widely adopted.

. .. .

DAY FORTY SEVEN :: WEDNESDAY
OCTOBER 29, 2008
"Do what you can, with what you have, where you are."
— Theodore Roosevelt, 26th American President, (1885-1919)

Today is my lecture "Saudi Arabia in Religious-Social Transition," in the lecture series on Islam, *Intellectuals and Ideology*, sponsored by the Dean's Special Activities Fund, the Political Science, Theology, and Islamic World Studies Departments. Over forty students and a few faculty members attended this lecture, and they were interested to hear about Saudi Arabia from a Saudi professor rather than hearing it from non-Saudis.

Here is a summary of my lecture. At the beginning of Muhammad ibn Abdulwahhab's reformation, scholars and mainstream Muslim societies throughout the Muslim World rejected his ideas. For many reasons, Wahhabism, in its early stages, appeared awkward and was not accepted. Even today, it is still unwelcome in many Muslim countries, although it is practiced by most people residing in Saudi Arabia. The arguments against the Wahhabism can be divided into two main categories: politics and theology.

In regard to politics, objections are raised that relate to seeking independence from the Ottoman Empire, and considering most of the Islamic countries as Non-Islamic states, thereby promoting Jihad (holy war) against them. Theological arguments suggest that Wahhabism is mainly practicing Ijtihad (e.g., disregarding the four legal doctrines), and claiming that certain behavior practiced by Muslims will equalize them with infidels. These behaviors include, but are not limited to, seeking blessing from dead Sufi imams, and believing in the twelve Imams of Shi'a.

Many historians and religious scholars have pursued their research of a political argument against Wahhabism unfairly. Muhammad Ali of Egypt was in charge of the military during the Ottoman Empire and the Ottoman caliph authorized him to prevent any movements against the Empire in the Arabian Peninsula. Because of his position, it can be assumed that Egyptian historians in particular were unreliable in their interpretation of Wahhabism. In general, contemporary Egyptian authors who wrote about Wahhabism, were very harsh.

Wahhabism had one major obstacle to overcome. How could they allow themselves to fight against the Muslim caliph and still secede from him? The main excuse Wahhabis used to justify their war against the Ottoman Empire was that Najd, modern-day Riyadh, was not controlled or governed by the Ottomans. Additionally, the Ottoman Empire was not practicing Islam, and therefore could lawfully establish a new Islamic political identity. My lecture focused on the theological arguments from this point on.

In order to understand the Wahhabi Movement, I introduced a short biography of ibn Abdulwahhab, including a bibliography of his works, particularly his magnum opus: Kitab at-Tawheed. I then described the reactions of local religious scholars to Wahhabism in three categories: total rejection, initial rejection followed by acceptance under political pressure, and total acceptance. Scholars who totally rejected Wahhabism joined its opponents in using all available means to demolish it. Among those who rejected it initially, were some who eventually became convinced by Wahabis' arguments or political pressure. The last group were those who accepted Wahhabism and were supportive of it in debates, scholarly writing, and in war.

The local scholars of that time provided the strongest arguments against Wahhabism, especially ibn Abdulwahhab's brother, Sulaiman, who was the judge of his city. Thus, Sulaiman's writing is essential to understand the flaws of Wahhabism. Other local scholars joined Sulaiman, including the well known scholar Sulaiman ibn Suhaim. I also covered Hamad ibn Mua'mmar, a famous student of ibn Abdulwahhab and the most knowledgeable defender of Wahhabism.

The Loyola Phoenix newspaper interviewed me after the lecture and asked me several questions that I am listing here with my answers:

> *Phoenix Reporter:* What is the mission or goal of your time as a Fulbright Scholar here at Loyola?

> *Response:* Loyola University is a Jesuit university and my university in Saudi Arabia, Imam Muhammad ibn Saud Islamic University is one of the leading Islamic universities in the Muslim World. My goal in the Fulbright Program is to foster interfaith work by building bridges between Islamic institutions and other institutions in the U.S.

> *Phoenix Reporter:* Your presentation focused on the history of Saudi Arabian politics. Do you see an understanding of history to be necessary to understand the events of today?

99

Response: Change in Saudi society has always been influenced by history and the surrounding circumstances which now extend to a global scale. Due to historical developments including issues such as Saudi Arabia's ascension to prominence in a global economy, our nation joining others in facing challenges including environmental problems, poverty, terrorism, and conflict. Toward these ends, King Abdullah of Saudi Arabia is committed to promoting peace, engaging in interfaith dialogue and addressing other global problems.

Phoenix Reporter: Can you further expand on your remarks that all Americans seem to care about in regards to Saudi Arabia is Wahhabism and oil?

Response: When Saudi Arabia is mentioned in American media, it is always linked with oil. The label Wahhabism is not understood by many Americans. The brand of Wahhabism that began around 1750 has changed overtime, so what began as an extremist movement has now become a more politically diverse group, including some moderate elements. In Saudi Arabia, we also have many other interests beyond politics and religion including art, sports, culture, history, poetry, and much more.

Phoenix Reporter: Is "change" as much of a buzzword these days in Saudi Arabia as it is in the United States?

Response: The Saudi Government is promoting the idea of change and progress and the people are beginning to accept this message and pursue these ends.

Much to my surprise, none of these questions and answers was printed in *The Phoenix*. Instead, they printed statements from my lecture without even asking for my permission. One should be more careful when dealing with media, not only in America but everywhere.

. . . .

DAY FORTY EIGHT :: THURSDAY
OCTOBER 30, 2008
"Every generation needs a new revolution."
— Thomas Jefferson, 3rd American President, (1743-1826)

Alexander Scott joined me in the panel at Loyola and then arranged for me to visit the Lutheran School of Theology in Chicago. On our way there, Scott showed me Farrakhan's home as we were in that neighborhood. He also mentioned that Barack Obama lived in the same neighborhood. As he was pointing at Obama's home, four police cars suddenly came out of that driveway. There was Obama in the last car; we waved. Although Scott was not less surprised than I, he smiled and joked, "See, I arranged with Obama to come out at this time to give you a chance to greet him during your program in Chicago."

The seminar I participated in ran from 2:30 p.m. until 5:00 p.m.; it was about the Role of Religious Leaders. My speech was about youth leadership. Every generation has its' own style, thoughts, needs, and thus its own leaders. It is wise to mentor the young leaders instead of directing them. Older leaders may imply their views which are based on perception and might be outdated especially in times like these when societies are changing dramatically.

. . . .

DAY FORTY NINE :: FRIDAY
OCTOBER 31, 2008
"Character is what you are in the dark."

— Dwight Moody, American Evangelist, (1837-1899)

Tonight is Halloween, which is viewed differently religiously and socially. Most Americans consider Halloween as a secular celebration. Kids wear customs and go trick-or-treating with their parents as escorts. Young people usually host costume parties and have lots of fun. Religious people view Halloween differently, some consider it to be a Pagan celebration that should not be celebrated, which seems to be the Islamic and Judaic position, while others see it as a secular celebration that is not harmful if kids have fun wearing weird clothes on that day. Like many other occasions, Halloween turns into a big business opportunity. On Halloween, TV channels present horror movies, and shops promote scary movies and books related to Halloween. There are several games traditionally associated with Halloween parties. One common game is bobbing for apples, in which apples float in a tub or a large basin that is filled with water and the participants must use their teeth to remove an apple from the basin. Another common game involves hanging up syrup-coated scones by strings; these must be eaten without using hands while they remain attached to the string, an activity that inevitably leads to a very sticky face. I used to play this game in Saudi Arabia when I was a child, and I never knew that it is related to Halloween.

Chapter 5

"*I have a dream that my four little children will one day live in a nation where they will not be judged by the color of their skin, but by the content of their character.*"

Martin Luther King Jr., AMERICAN ACTIVIST, (1929-1968)

. . ..

DAY FIFTY :: SATURDAY
NOVEMBER 1, 2008
"A man who stands for nothing will fall for anything."
— Malcolm X, American activist, (1925-1965)

The American Academy of Religion (AAR) has over 10,000 members who teach in approximately 1,500 colleges, universities, seminaries, and schools in North America and abroad. The Academy is dedicated to furthering knowledge of religion and religious institutions in all their forms and manifestations. This goal is accomplished through Academy-wide and regional conferences and meetings, publications, programs, and membership services. The AAR annual conference at Chicago Hilton Tower was an excellent opportunity for me to meet with scholars from all religious disciplines. I had dinner with the Islamic Studies group at Riza Persian restaurant. During the dinner I met with over a hundred scholars specializing in Islamic Studies. I am still in touch with several of them. These conferences and organizations are in all fields of sciences, allowing American professors to meet one another as well as meet with professors from all over the world. They keep themselves up-to-date by joining theses academic associations and following their publications. In the recent years, scientific associations begin to take their place in Saudi Arabia and they are doing well.

103

. . ..

DAY FIFTY ONE :: SUNDAY
NOVEMBER 2, 2008
"I have seen the science I worshiped, and the aircraft I loved, destroying the civilization I expected them to serve."
— Charles Lindbergh, American Aviator, (1902-1974)

None of the panels at the AAR interested me today more than the discussions I had with several smart graduate students. We were discussing three main topics, one of which was the conflict between Islamic Law and the Modern State. I explained to them the central argument of my article on this topic; "Can Islamic Law and the modern state peacefully co-exist or are these institutions inherently contradictory?" In my article, I suggest that since legal and political reforms began in the 19th Century, when the Nation-State emerged in the Near and Middle East and the *Shari'a* was largely supplanted by its law, this has been a perennial issue of intellectuals and statesmen. From the collapse of the Ottoman Empire to American hegemony, the problem of negotiating religious and legal authority with the State has been of dominant concern. My paper broadly identified and evaluated how a spectrum of political and religious leaders have attempted to settle this disagreement until the present, from the radical rejection of Western legal and political forms to the outright abandonment of Islamic Law. Moving towards a greater consensus, the paper also offered a nascent solution to the impasse between Shari'a and the modern state, based upon a new reading of prophetic tradition which promises an evolutionary approach to Islamic statecraft.

To understand the modern state better, it is useful to study the formation of the U.S. as an example of the modern state. America was originally colonized by British settlers that received land from the British monarchy. One famous example is William Penn (1644-1718) who received a large grant from Charles II to form a colony on the new continent. Penn had become a member of the Quakers, a radical reformation group that emphasized the internal revelation of God in guiding one's life and rejected any final authority of the government. Because he had been jailed and persecuted for his beliefs, he wanted to make his colony a safe place for similar Christian sects. He gave plots of land to immigrating families and built the city of Philadelphia near the coast. Philadelphia quickly became one of the first major cities in America and was the site of the Continental Congress where America declared its independence.

Although America had been established as a series of British colonies, the British government had instituted several unpopular laws that the colonists felt were exploitive. Once the French-Indian War had ended in 1763, Britain felt that the colonies should help pay for the military costs to defend them against France's attempt to extend its colonial boundaries. In 1765, Britain tried to establish the Stamp Act, placing a tax on all printed pages in America. Americans widely denounced this law, responding with the famous slogan "No taxation without representation." Americans began to claim that without a democratically elected presence in Britain, they could not lawfully be forced to support the government. The unpopularity of the law resulted in its repeal. The British reacted by imposing several taxes on imports, and instituting laws that punished colonies that refused to allow British troops to stay in their homes. The tax on tea, combined with a tax repeal that made British tea cheaper than other kinds, resulted in an attack on East India Tea Company ships in 1773, when a mob raided the ships and threw the tea overboard. The violent outburst of The Boston Tea Party represented widespread resentment towards British legislation that culminated in the First Continental Congress in 1774. Here delegates from every colony except Georgia criticized British interference and organized a boycott against British trade. The Congress eventually prompted British forces to try to seize colonial ammunition holdings at Concord and Lexington in April, 1775; the colonists defended their territory which resulted in victory over the British in the first battle of the American Revolution.

In May of 1775, the Second Continental Congress met. In June, they appointed

George Washington (1732-1799) as Commander-in-chief of the Continental Army, the day after it voted the Army into existence. Washington, a Virginian, served as a soldier in the French-Indian Wars, and was well-known and respected throughout the colonies for the strength of his character and his public critique of British policy. The colonies had now come together under his leadership to combat British military suppression, but it was not until the following year that colonies initiated a radical break from the British.

In July of 1776, the Congress passed the Declaration of Independence, which announced the formation of an independent nation, America, and descriptions of liberty. The first draft of the Declaration of Independence had been written by Thomas Jefferson (1743-1826), a brilliant, well-educated Virginian who studied and wrote on a vast number of subjects throughout his life. His major treatise, written in 1774, *Summary View of the Rights of British America*, laid out the case for the British colonies. After passages referring to the equality of all men were removed, due to objections from the South Carolina Delegation, the Declaration was ratified and the United States of America was formed.

105

. . . .

DAY FIFTY TWO :: MONDAY
NOVEMBER 3, 2008
"If you believe that feeling bad or worrying long enough will change a past or future event, then you are residing on another planet with a different reality system."
— William James, American psychologist and philosopher, (1842-1910)

There were thousands of people at AAR from different backgrounds and religions, most of them are Christians, so I find it appropriate to introduce the history of Christianity from a Christian perspective, which differs slightly from the Islamic perspective. Two thousand years ago, Christianity began as a movement made up primarily of Jews in ancient Palestine. Its founders were disciples (i.e., followers) of Jesus of Nazareth, who lived roughly between 4 BCE and 37 CE. He was born the son of a carpenter and eventually became a well-known religious teacher. As a teacher, Jesus was both respected and controversial. His fame spread throughout the Mediterranean world, where he was known as a powerful miracle-worker and an authoritative teacher. But a number of his teachings were considered offensive by the religious leaders of his Jewish community.

Christians claim that Jesus said that God was his "Father," that he said, "I and the Father are one," and that he preached against the hypocrisy that he observed in the religious leaders. He called them "white-washed tombs," claiming that their "outside" was clean but their "inside" was full of decay. According to the Gospel accounts of Jesus' life, the Jewish leaders were driven by jealousy to stop Jesus from teaching. In an attempt to carry out their plans, these leaders put Jesus on trial and declared him guilty

of cursing God. They also brought him before the Roman authorities, claiming that Jesus was an insurrectionist who had called himself "King of the Jews." Although the Roman leader, Pontius Pilate, found Jesus guilty of no crime, he was forced to maintain order by allowing Jesus to be crucified, hung on a cross to die. Three days after his death, the followers of Jesus encountered him alive.

Together the life, death, and resurrection of Jesus form the central idea of Christianity. Through his obedience, even in death, and his vindication in resurrection, Jesus paved the way for others to live in loving, hope-filled intimacy with God. For Muslims, Jesus was not crucified, as God elevated him to Heaven and someone else who looks like Jesus was put on the cross. Muslims also believe that Jesus will come back before the Judgment Day and will lead all believers to the right path, and to Heaven.

. . ..

DAY FIFTY THREE :: TUESDAY
NOVEMBER 4, 2008
"I have a dream that my four little children will one day live in a nation where they will not be judged by the color of their skin, but by the content of their character."
— Martin Luther King Jr., American activist, (1929-1968)

Election Day. The American public knows history is in the making, and spirits are high. In general, Americans vote for candidates in either the Democratic or Republican Party. Parties are groups that share general views on policies and

*Together the life, death, and resurrection of Jesus
form the central idea of Christianity.*

issues. Not everyone in a party agrees with everything the party says; as an example, some rural Democrats in Pennsylvania and Ohio are focused on the government supporting labor and protecting workers from being exploited by their employers whereas some educated Democrats in California are more interested in helping the poor and working against racism. But each party agrees broadly on the role the government should play in everyday life, and comes together as a group to decide on candidates, deliberate issues, and to collect and distribute money.

Both major political parties in American politics, the Democrats and the Republicans claim Thomas Jefferson's Democratic Republican Party as their ancestor. The modern Democratic National Committee came into existence in 1848, and the first Democratic President was Woodrow Wilson (1856-1924). Democrats believe that the government should work for the social good, support the poor and the elderly, and fund education and cultural development. They think that the government should regulate businesses to prevent abuses, and that government should allow many moral viewpoints.

The Republican Party was founded in 1854 to combat slavery and provide free land to Western settlers. The first Republican President was Abraham Lincoln (1809-1865). Contemporary Republicans think that the government should be as small as possible, not passing many laws or having many social programs, but should allow individuals and private businesses to solve problems without legal interference. They think that markets distribute wealth best if they are not inhibited by laws, and they want to preserve traditional and conservative moral viewpoints.

Americans do not have to belong to either of these two parties. Some people are Independents, combining qualities of both parties. Other people belong to what are called "third parties," which just means a large party which is not one of the major two, like the Green Party or the Libertarians. Belonging to a party only means that a person supports the party's goals, will sometimes give money, and volunteer their time to help the candidates.

Barack Obama (1961-) was elected as the forty-fourth President of the U.S. and belongs to the Democratic Party. He is the son of a White American mother and a Kenyan father. He served in the state senate, and then as an Illinois congressional senator. He became a national figure as a result of his acclaimed speech during the 2004 Democratic Convention. He began running for President in 2007. He fought a long, difficult primary campaign against both Sen. Hillary Clinton and Sen. John Edwards, who both seemed initially more likely to become the Democratic candidate. In 2008, he ran in a close race against Republican Sen. John McCain until the economy started faltering. After that, polls tilted in his favor, and on Election Day, he became the first African American President.

On the election night, friends invited me to go to hear Obama's acceptance speech,

107

but the venue was so crowded that I preferred to accept another invitation to go to William's home to watch the election results and have dinner with his family and friends. It is amazing how kids know so much about the election; they knew the parties and the states' preferences between Republicans and Democrats as well as which were the swing states. There are 50 states and 1 district in total. In addition to being a historic turning point not only for Americans and non-Americans, it was just plain fun to watch the last few hours of the election.

. . . .

DAY FIFTY FOUR :: WEDNESDAY
NOVEMBER 5, 2008
"Good people are good because they've come to wisdom through failure. We get very little wisdom from success."

— William Saroyan, American writer, (1908-1981)

I usually have lunch with Dennis Martin on Wednesday; today we discussed Vatican II. Vatican II represents a foundational belief for Catholic Christians that the church is always being actively reformed. The application of Christian doctrine is not carved in stone, it is living and changing. It is not static, but dynamic; it is as living as the very people who make up the church. As such, new claims are periodically made by the churches that reflect epistemological developments within both Christianity and society at large. When leaders of the church gather in an official meeting to decide on

CHAPTER V

Historic election

Barack Obama's election as the forty-fourth President of the U.S. was a historical turning point, for Americans and non-Americans.

new theological formulations, the assembly is referred to as a "council."

One of the most transformative councils in the last several centuries was held in the 1960s at the Vatican in Rome. Because it was the second such gathering at this location, it is entitled simply the "Second Vatican Council." This meeting, opened by Pope John XXIII in 1962 and closed by Pope Paul VI in 1965, was held to discuss such important subjects as the nature of the church, the relation of Christianity to other religions, the relation of Catholicism to other Christian denominations, and the posture that should be maintained by the Church in response to modernity. It resulted in four "constitutions," nine "decrees," and three "declarations," all of which were put forward as official church teachings. The primary claims made by these documents can be summarized in relation to three categories: the nature of the church, the method of worship in the Catholic community, and divine revelation in Christian scripture.

109

The nature of the church was radically redefined by Vatican II. Prior to this council, the Catholic Church held that it was 'the' one, true church and those non-Catholics were refused God's grace, because they were outside of the true church. Yet, in Vatican II a more inclusive understanding of church was inaugurated. In the document entitled "The Dogmatic Constitution of the Church," or *Lumen Gentium*, the true church is said to subsist in the Catholic church, but it maintains nevertheless, "many elements of sanctification and of truth are found outside its visible confines" (*Lumen Gentium*, 15-16). Moreover, because God's desire is to save people, not just individuals, all human beings are called to belong to the church and may be considered to do so, even if they are not baptized into the Catholic Church. In this way, not only other Christians — Protestants and Eastern Orthodox — but also people of other religions — Jews and Muslims — are said to partake in a mystical communion with the Catholic Church.

The method of worship in the Catholic community, or liturgy, was also changed by the decisions of Vatican II. Prior to these declarations, a priest performed the ceremonies of the Catholic mass in Latin, a practice that upheld the respect that should surround worship, but that did not allow non-Latin-speaking people to participate fully in their understanding. Thus, in the "Constitution on Sacred Liturgy" or *Sacrosanctum Concilium*, the church declared, "all the faithful should be led to that fully conscious and active participation in liturgical celebrations which is demanded by the very nature of the liturgy" (*Sacrosanctum Concilium*, 14). Priests followed this institution by incorporating the use of indigenous languages into the liturgical ceremonies. Finally, the church's belief in the importance of Christian scripture as a resource for constructing theology and understanding divine revelation was elevated in such a way that many Catholics began studying the Bible anew. These changes encouraged scholars to continue producing translations of the Bible in the vernacular of the people. This in turn encouraged Bible studies among both clergy and laity. Catholic leaders observed a renewed interest in scripture which allowed the denomination as a whole to engage with critical scholarship of biblical texts, and opened a new course of dialogue with Protestants about their foundational claim that the Bible alone contains everything the Christian needs for faith and practice.

. . ..

DAY FIFTY FIVE :: THURSDAY
NOVEMBER 6, 2008
"O Lord, help me not to despise or oppose what I do not understand."
— William Penn, American founder of Pennsylvania, (1644-1718)

Dennis Martin and I continued our interfaith dialogue.

Perhaps the most distinguishing characteristic of Christianity and the most difficult to understand is its belief in the "trinity." In its most basic expression, the trinity concept is explained as the Creator God as one in essence and three in person. This teaching did not develop immediately in Christian history but eventually gained expression as the church interpreted Jesus' teachings in light of the Judaism it inherited.

Like Islam, Judaism taught that God is one. Jews prayed, "Hear, O Israel, the Lord our God, the Lord is One!" The earliest expressions of Christianity maintained the truth of this doctrine but also reinterpreted it. Basing their teachings on the claim that Jesus was an equal of God, the founders of Christianity taught the divinity of Jesus, saying that Jesus existed "in the beginning," was "with God" and "was God." Further, Jesus himself promised that after his death a "counselor" would continue to instruct his followers and would, in-fact, be the very presence of Jesus in their hearts.

In an attempt to synthesize these mysteriously divergent teachings, Christian theologians eventually formulated the doctrine of the trinity. Adopting the language of Jesus, they differentiated within the one God three "persons" or separate existences: the father, who is the source of all that exists; the Son, who is the mediator between the father and creation; and, the spirit who is the presence of God in creation. According to the Christian Bible, God *is* love. Because the love that is God is so magnificently profound, the three are united indistinguishably in essence, even while they are differentiated in personhood. The spirit is an ambiguous concept. In the Quran, when it was mentioned, God says "They ask thee concerning the spirit. Say: 'The spirit by command of my Lord: of knowledge it is only a little that is communicated to you.'"

The Bible itself is a central source of authority for Christians. As such, the earliest Christians' beliefs about God's new activity in the person of Jesus were rooted in the religious tradition and language of Judaism. The religious writings that Christians inherited from the Jews form the first part of the Christian scriptures. They are called the

Old Testament, or Old Covenant, since most Christians believe that with the coming of Jesus, a new covenant was established between God and His people. The scriptural texts that are specifically Christian, those that were written after Jesus' life and ministry, are referred to as the New Testament, or New Covenant. Together, the Old Testament and the New Testament make up the Christian Bible.

As is suggested by their titles, the centralizing theme of these writings can be summed up in terms of a relational covenant between God and His people, a relationship that is not without conflict. Whereas God consistently reached out in love, God's people consistently rejected God's loving pursuit and, in turn, suffered the consequences of their disobedience. Yet the message of brokenness was never without hope. Throughout the Old Testament, words of judgment were always accompanied with words of redemption. In the last verse of the last book of the Old Testament, a prophet was promised who would initiate a final, nationwide return to the precepts that God had established for the Jews. This could be what Muslims believe to be the foretelling of Prophet Muhammad, peace be upon him, as the promised prophet.

The Christian Scriptures identified Jesus as the one who would save them from their sins by means of his perfect, covenantal relationship with God. The writings of these scriptures can be divided into five sections: (1) four historical accounts of Jesus life, (2) one historical account of the church's beginnings, (3) the instructional writings of Paul the Apostle, (4) instructional writings by other early Christian leaders, and (5) a prophetic anticipation of the end of the world and the beginning of the afterlife.

A key concept in Christianity is salvation. Basing their theology on the biblical account of creation, Christians maintain that the Earth and its inhabitants were originally created in perfect harmony with each other, with Earth, and with God. In the first chapter of Genesis, the author portrayed this perfection by saying, "God saw all that had been made, and it was very good." Yet it is according to the same story that, not long after creation was declared good, humans made decisions that disrupted this peace. Adam and Eve, the first man and woman in the book of Genesis, attempted to become like God. They were unsatisfied with their created status and attempted to elevate themselves to the level of their Creator. Genesis symbolically refers to this event as their eating fruit from "the tree of the knowledge of good and evil." Historically, Christians have named this event "original sin."

For Muslims, the Quran narrates this story stating that Adam and Eve were trying to eat from the tree of eternity. However, in the Quran, Adam was held accountable for his sin and it was not transferred to his children, thus, people are free of sin until they commit their own sins to which they will be held accountable individually.

As a result of this decision, a decision which Christians maintain is shared by the whole human race, that original harmony was lost. The peace between humans was replaced with competition; the fruitful harmony they enjoyed with the Earth was

111

replaced with a need to work the ground for produce; and the loving relationship that existed between humans and God was damaged. Yet the Christian story does not stop there. The Gospel of John says that "God so loved the world that he gave his only begotten Son" for its salvation: it is through the life, death, and resurrection of Jesus that God began to recreate original harmony. The Christian testament claims, further, that Jesus lived in perfect peace with God; that in him "all created things hold together;" and that his life of love has initiated the creation of a new human race that will be characterized by love. He is, therefore, called "the second Adam," since it is in him that all three areas of disharmony, human to human, human to Earth, and human to God, are considered to be reestablished or recreated in peace.

For Muslims, the concept of "original sin" is not the same, thus they did not need another Adam to start over. They needed a revelation from God to teach them how to obey, be forgiven and return to eternal life in Heaven.

. . . .

DAY FIFTY SIX: FRIDAY
November 7, 2008
"Law not served by power is an illusion; but power not ruled by law is a menace which our nuclear age cannot afford."

— Arthur J. Goldberg, American judge, (1908-1990)

Another interesting conversation and reflection with Dennis Martin on Western public religious dynamics lasted for about an hour today. Dennis concludes that his main point was based on the assumption that most of my conversation partners during my six weeks here will be political and religious post-modern liberals. Almost no one in American universities comes either from hard-line Enlightenment rationalism or from pre-Enlightenment traditionalism. Universities are 'hothouse' environments from which conservative or traditional thought is excluded. After many years of this trend, conservatives went out and established their own research centers; the various conservative Washington think tanks: The Heritage Institute, Ethics and Public Policy Center, etc. Many people in the West think that what Islam needs to do is to adopt Western Enlightenment thinking. Dennis is suggesting that the older traditions of the West have much to offer that is more amenable to Islam than either modern or postmodern Western thinking.

Dennis thinks what was happening here is that Europeans are realizing, after encountering other cultures intensely, that persuading everyone to share universal principles simply won't work. It is far better to bite the bullet and recognize that, in the end, each group simply tries to universalize its own parochial beliefs and impose them on the rest of the world. So it is about power and power alone, after all. Postmodernism in the 20ᵗʰ Century represents the logical conclusion that if the proposed universal moral systems turn out to be merely projections from this or that religious, economic, class, or racial group, then none of them are universally compelling. In this view, Marxism names economic power struggle as the engine that drives history. Feminism names the gender power struggle as the engine. Black Liberation theology chooses race. These approaches dominate most universities, including Loyola. These power struggle theories are central in required reading for doctoral students in theology. Postmodern "it's all about power" thinking now governs large segments of Western culture.

Now, as for the alternatives: there are two basic types of conservative ideologies in the West today. One is often called "neo-conservative" but that label is really not helpful. Dennis called them "common-good free-market conservatives." Basically, they believe that the original American founding was based on acceptance of a free-market individualism that placed common good limits or brakes on laissez-faire capitalism. The other type is called "paleo-conservatives." They distrust neo-conservatives because they believe that the appeal to free-markets by the neo-conservatives is really just another version of laissez-faire capitalism that lets business dominate everyone to the detriment of the poor and average person. They blame the Jacobins of the French Revolution for destroying all the old institutions and structures that took care of the common-good and they think that laissez-faire capitalism, today globalized, continues that destructive Jacobinism.

Dennis believes that a nation like Saudi Arabia, which wishes to hold religion central in its political life, needs to take account of the various forms of traditionalist or conservative thinking that can be found in the West. The reigning ideology on university campuses in the West reduces everything to a power struggle and, in the long run, that's a formula for disaster. That's what produced Stalin, Mao, and Hitler. And it will corrupt Islam as well if it takes hold.

Yet, I have another solution for the political-religious struggle, which I presented in my lecture at the Community Builder of North Chicago about Muslim minorities living in non-Islamic states. To begin with, Islam is not against progress, rather they are quite compatible and, progress consequently represents a reformulation of Islamic doctrine. In terms of modern thought, it is not only possible but desirable. The question then is how to relate the past to the present and the future in a positive and meaningful way; how to become modern and remain Muslim at the same time. The question is how to be a Muslim and live under non-Islamic rule? Similar to this is what the Jews have been through for the last four centuries when they established a law in the condition of living under a foreign government. Basically, all that Muslims have to believe includes the six pillars of faith, i.e., believing in God, angels, holy books meaning the Torah, Bible and Quran, the prophets including Noah, Abraham,

113

Moses, Jesus, and Muhammad, peace be upon them all. In addition Muslims have to practice the five pillars of Islam, i.e., testimony of faith, praying five times a day, fasting the month of Ramadan, paying the alms-tax and making the pilgrimage to Mecca in Saudi Arabia if they are able to. For family law, they have to implement Islamic teachings which extend to their social lives. As for the penal law and political issues, Muslims are not obliged to apply any of them in a non-Islamic state.

. . . .

DAY FIFTY SEVEN :: SATURDAY
NOVEMBER 8, 2008
"Those who sacrifice liberty for security deserve neither."
— Benjamin Franklin, American statesman, (1706-1790)

When I arrived in Denver I took a shuttle to the Hotel. The U.S. transportation system is very convenient. Even if a traveler does not arrange for a pick-up, he can easily find his way with different kinds of public transportation. In the shuttle there were few Americans, one was of Jewish origin, living in CA but she was visiting her relatives in Denver. The others were a couple living in the neighborhood of my hotel. We had a very nice conversation over about an hour from the airport to the hotel. What I like about discussing national topics with Americans is their willingness to use critical thinking to discuss both negative and positive situations in the U.S. After I told them about my ICAP program and my plan to write a book about American culture and religious diversity, they happily shared with me their opinions about various topics, one of which was equality.

The United States Declaration of Independence was signed at historic Independence Hall in Philadelphia, PA, on July 4, 1776.

One of the founding principles of the United States is equality before the law, meaning that everyone has the same rights and the same opportunities. The Declaration of Independence affirms that the creator of humanity has created each of them equal. The drafters of the Constitution did not want to have the same aristocratic class or ruling monarch that England had. They tried to extend the rule of law to cover every citizen, so that any one person would not be exempt from the law or have special rights. But everyone was not equal from the beginning, and it has taken a long time for America to work towards universal equality.

African Americans remained slaves in early America. Even after the Civil War ended slavery as an institution, Black people were segregated, forced to use separate schools, living areas, restaurants, work menial jobs, and were denigrated by White people. Black people did not gain full legal protection until the 1960s.

115

Women were never enslaved, but they were prevented from owning property and were not offered many of the opportunities that men had. They were unable to vote until the passage of the 19th Amendment. Today, Americans are trying to expand the representation of women at higher levels of business, government, and academia, and to fix disparities in pay and opportunity. Women are currently paid anywhere from 69% to 80% of what men are paid. Women's groups support the legalization of abortion, paid maternity leave, and the provision of daycare to allow women to pursue careers while having families. In the past, women in Saudi Arabia were limited to care-taking type roles such as administrative support, nursing and school teachers but, in recent years, several government and private initiatives have paved new roads for women, allowing them to become full participants in the marketplace. However, because the society still maintains a strong traditional patriarchal family structure where women are rarely the primary wage-earners of a household, they may not earn as much as their male counterparts, depending on their fields.

Another more recent controversy in America was over the rights of homosexual couples to marry, which many see as an equal rights problem. However, several religious groups oppose legal condoning of homosexuality, since they believe it to be immoral. Recently, the California Supreme Court declared bans on gay marriage to be unconstitutional. Several thousand gay couples got married before Proposition 8, an amendment to the California state constitution that defined marriage as a union between a man and a woman, was voted on during the 2008 Election. Proposition 8, and similar laws in Arizona and Florida, was narrowly voted in, leaving only Massachusetts and Connecticut as states that allow gay marriage.

Chapter 6

"*Before you contradict an old man, my fair friend, you should endeavor to understand him.*"

George Santayana, American philosopher, (1863-1952)

. . ..

DAY FIFTY EIGHT : SUNDAY
NOVEMBER 9, 2008
"A man may die, nations may rise and fall, but an idea lives on."
————John F. Kennedy, 35th American President, (1917-1963)

For this reunion of our Fulbright ICAP group, the State Department had arranged for us to study the history of Native Americans as taught by Native Americans themselves. Tink Tinker, a Native American leader in Denver and an ordained Lutheran pastor, was our host at Illif University. He welcomed us by explaining how Native American names have meaning that guide life; Tink means "walks between two worlds" for example. During this weekend we would walk among several worlds: the Native American one alongside each of our own indigenous cultures, Malaysian, Indonesian, French, Lebanese, Saudi Arabian, Iranian, British, Pakistani, eastern Indian, and African. And overlaid on all of these would be our globalized cultural world in which we speak English and use the analytic tools of academia to try and understand one another. Tink knew from his walk between worlds what we were up against and he began our time together with a spiritual song, the Eagle song, to help loosen our preconceptions:

> *Mea toka hea*
> *hape toac hee elo*
> *Wamle glash cabwa*
> *Wela eelora heee*
>
> *To sing to our eagle*
> *to come please us*
> *someone is coming first*
> *man is coming*
> *and eagle is coming to give us hope*

Then Paul, a spiritual leader among Native Americans, recited their prayer in their language then he translated it as follows:

Great grandfather, come together with us today and gather these people from different lands and different experiences. Help us understand these experiences that each of us brings from our own backgrounds. We thank you for bringing us together and letting us share today. As we go on today help us, guide us, and may we be touched by your guidance.

After the prayers, Tink asked each of us to introduce ourselves, and we did. Few Native Americans were present; one of them was named "small bear," then when she got older, they began calling her "old woman bear sitting next to the creator." Thank goodness, though, she said we could call her Sharon, her American name. After the introductions, Tink handed out the program from left to right; I learned that Americans call this direction clockwise, but the Native Americans would say Sunwise.

In spite of the American's effort to convert Native Americans to not only their religion, but to their culture as well, Native Americans have managed to keep their culture alive. Today's presentation introduced us to four major characteristics in contradistinction to the overlay of American culture in general. These characteristics include: 1) the interrelationship of all life, 2) communitarianism, 3) spatiality, and 4) the use of and reverence for land.

In Native American teaching, there are two divisions on this world, the sky and the earth. Within these two realms, all of life is interrelated, even rocks and rivers, which Tink illustrated with a story. He had been collecting rocks with some friends who were scientists and theologians. When he explained to them that the twenty-four rocks they had just collected had agreed to come along with them, they looked at him with skepticism. Tink feels one must be born Native American to understand, especially given that their languages do not include a word for "believe." His friends are skeptical when they think Tink believes in rocks or rivers. But Tink says the native language speaks more of being aware or conscious of the life that is in all things. Even when a tree is felled for example, the person felling the tree speaks to the tree, thanking it for its life, explaining how it will be used to further life in the building of a fire or of a home. They do not have words for "war" or "punishment" even though they have been labeled as warriors. Again, the reverence for all life that forms their identity is at work. If a child or a tribe member is out of sync with this deep reverence, usually a look or a gentle reminder is enough to bring the community back into harmony as the one who has torn the fabric can sense mending is needed. They also use a form of sign language which has about thirty-thousand concepts possible for communication.

This first understanding of how all of life is connected leads to the second cultural difference that is essential for Native Americans. They are communitarians with far less of an emphasis on American individualism than exists in mainstream America. In American society, the rights of the individual are more important than the rights of a group. When this preconception is forced onto the tribal communities of the Native Americans, their social cohesion is threatened. I would add that this same difference and misunderstanding has contributed to why America has been less successful than they had hoped in Iraq. They are trying to bring Muslims who are Sunni, Shi'i, and Kurds under one state when each of these groups want to maintain their political identities based on their ethnic group sense. They do not want to be unified beneath a state banner.

In the communitarian life of the Native Americans, ceremonies offer the social cohesion that helps sustain this group identity over an individual one, while maintaining full recognition of the person's individuality. For example, coming of age ceremonies for girls and boys allow them each to take an individual place within the adult community, but with a powerful sense of belonging to a whole greater than their individual selves. Other ceremonies exist for the changes of the season, for working with medicine, for marriage, birth, and death.

One strong example of ceremonies that strengthen the sense of community spirituality and identity are those associated with ritual dances. The sun dance, for example, is done for four days without water in order to induce a trance-like state in which visions and guidance are received. Tink was clear to emphasize that these ceremonies differ from tribe to tribe, further reinforcing the value of community.

There are some basic assumptions, however, about their community practices. Native Americans practice a respect for spatiality that is only beginning to be understood by the larger American culture. Circles are important. When a ceremonial circle is formed, attention is paid to where and how they run the circle. There are four directions that go from west to north to east and to south that represent courage, wisdom, strength, and generosity. Then Native Americans value three other directions: above, below, and where one is. The number seven then becomes significant in relation to other valuations of the rhythm of four: the four age cycles: birth, childhood, adult and old age; the four seasons, the four colors related to the four directions: red, black, yellow, and white.

The fourth and most important cultural difference between Native Americans and mainstream American culture is their dispute over territories and lands. Every piece of land is very important to the Native American. When Europeans arrived, they did not view the land to be owned by the Native Americans, and from the beginning much fighting and sorrow ensued. Andrew Jackson is the most hated American President in Native American history because he is blamed for ordering the genocide in the 1830s, which is known as "The Trail of Tears." The U.S. Army forced Native Americans to walk from south to north fifteen-hundred miles from their place of birth, their lifetime homes to a controlled reservation. Almost thirty percent of them died (about one-hundred-twenty-thousand), while American soldiers were riding their horses. American and English people justified their confiscation of the land on the basis that Natives had not improved the land by using new technologies to replace practices they had been doing for centuries.

During the question and answer period, Mohammad Ali asked Tink how he could be a Lutheran and Native American at the same time. Tink earned a Ph.D. in religion; he is fluent in Hebrew and Greek and has a respect for the culture surrounding Jesus and a respect for Jesus himself. In general though, he and many other Native Americans do not have respect for the church that grew out of the 4th Century evolution of the early Christian faith. Other faculty members at Illif University combine their original faith with different religions like Buddhism, Islam, and Judaism. Tink would never call himself a missionary because missionaries were indeed part of the Native American genocide,

119

but he does strive to bridge cultures through engaging in dialogue about his Native American spirituality and Christianity.

Ghassan made a comment about the similarity between Sufi tradition of practicing worship in a circle and the Native American's respect for circles. Also, he saw a similarity between communicating with natural objects and that according to Sufi tradition, Prophet Muhammad, peace be upon him, talked to animals and stones. Many Sufis have continued this tradition of communicating with nature.

Just as the Muslim World has not always accepted these Sufi practices, so too does the American government distrust some Native American religious practices. Although the Native American Freedom of Religion Act was passed in 1978, they have lost every single case that they brought to the American court system under this provision. Police have been known to interrupt any Indian ceremony and collect all of their sacred art and put it in museums. Controversies still exist over which ceremonies will be allowed.

Ziad and Professor Wasey raised questions about the future of Native Americans especially given the social change we see that Muslims have gone through after 9-11. They also wondered whether the election of an African American President would make a difference in respect to these minority practices. African Americans are seeing their dream of decades come true. So what is the dream and future of Native Americans?

Tink responded by saying that 50% of Native Americans are unemployed; on some of the reservations that number rises to 60% and 90% of the population. The life expectancy of Native Americans (except for one reservation near Los Angeles) is 44 years which is 20 years less than for the average American. 50% of Native American students drop out of high school and their subsequent income remains low. In addition, when Native Americans earn a degree in law or business, they will leave the community or tribe on a reservation or in a low-income neighborhood and will not, in general, think of serving or helping to bring members of the community along to a higher stage with them. Native Americans in the U.S. number about three million or 1% of the total population. In 1492, before the European invasion, Native Americans were 25 to 40 million. By the time Tink had finished giving us all these statistics, we were pretty clear about what Native Americans might dream of.

During the second session at Illif, Glenn Morris presented about the Indigenous Political System. He claimed that what he would share was not solely from him, but also from his grandfathers. He brought his sacred items to help him express his speech in an understandable way. To begin the discussion, Glenn asked us what image we had of Native Americans. We all agreed we carried the stereotype of the Native Americans as fierce warriors scalping the heads of Americans.

The Native American Paul spoke of how common the game of Cowboys and Indians was, with the cowboys always winning. He did not appreciate his own red skin when he played that game. When his mother and father divorced and his mother remarried a German man, he was excited because he thought he would turn White, but after many months passed, and he had not, he was disappointed that he would have to live with his red skin. Another Native American said she was not welcomed at school and they always asked her to deny that she was a Native American. She refused and was often beaten at school until they finally threw her out of school when she was sixteen. The Catholic sister at the school told her that she would go to Hell. This woman told us she had let this Catholic missionary know that if she, the Native American, would go to Hell because of her disbelief then the Catholic sister would meet her there because of her disrespectful behavior.

This prejudice against the Native Americans began in 1492 when Columbus arrived and wrote to his funders about the indigenous people, saying that he could defeat them with fifty men. Later on, Thomas Jefferson, William Henry, and others understood the Bible to mean native people were beasts when in Genesis 1:28 it states that God created Adam and Eve in his image and told them to multiply and supplant the Earth, its land, and its beasts. Europeans treated Native Americans as they did the buffalo, snakes, and other beasts and believed that they had no right to the land they were living on.

Again, in spite of these disrespectful stereotypes, Glenn tried to help us understand the Native American political system. One of the major principles is the seven-generation principle that says that Native Americans do not make any political decision until they think of its effect on the coming seven generations. Another principle is that women are involved in war decisions, expressing their opinions about whether the struggle or war that the men are going to wage is justified or not. In the indigenous society, their history and treaties are sacred and they are kept by women. They reason that a word is to an idea the same as the breath is to life; because women then give birth to the next generations and talk is a birth of words, then it is important for women to participate in these important choices and treaties of the nation. They trust that their future safety and happiness will be secure.

Glenn read a story written by Franklin, about a Native American meeting with a missionary. The missionary started to tell him about Adam and Eve, and how Adam disobeyed and ate the apple he was not supposed to eat. He described how this resulted in his children carrying his sin until Jesus came to be crucified in order to purify them, emphasizing how they must follow Jesus and understand the "original sin." Then the Native American replied saying, "Yes, I know how bad and sad it is to eat apple; they should have made cider out of it instead of eating it." Then the Native American told the missionary the story of the ancestor. The missionary said it is all fiction and unbelievable. The Native American said, we were educated to respect and believe others, but you were not.

◀ *Native Americans*

During the days we spent with Native Americans the most exciting time was when they performed their dances.

For Native Americans, it seems that even today, Americans believe that non-American land is genuine open country, free for Americans to invade. They still use the term "going off the reservation" to refer to Native Americans who leave their reservations. Some who would use this language would prefer that Native Americans stay on the reservations. Many Native American petitions for increased land rights are still denied.

Our third session today at Illif was about Women in Native American culture. We were able to learn much more about the place of women as Native Americans from three female presenters; Ann Erika or White Bird, Troy Lynn, and Sharon Venne.

Troy, from Mexico, started by telling us that women do hold much respect in the tribe, but that they often do so quietly, behind the scenes, while the men sit at the table having debates and discussion. The Native American women are starting to be involved in these discussions now, and bring a different dynamic to the issues discussed. Troy told us about her grandmother who refused to wear non-traditional clothes or speak English in her effort to sustain tribal communal customs. She was punished for her rebellion at the age of twelve. One day they washed her face with light soap and she lost her eyesight which she never regained. She remained faithful to her Native American spirituality until she died in the 1960s at the age of ninety.

Then Sharon, from Canada, explained more in detail about the value of the Native American sun dance which they have been doing from 1886 until 1956, when it was made illegal in Canada. Although the Canadian government tries to force them to stop, they continue to practice the ritual. In the rituals like the sun dance, men cannot start a dance by themselves; a woman must start the dance before the men can dance. Native American women are not allowed to hunt, because they give life, so they should not take life, but if they have to, then there are ceremonies they have to do before and after they hunt, asking for forgiveness and explaining why they must use the life in order to survive. For Sharon, women have been underestimated in America and Canada. And, in spite of respect for them within their own culture, Native American women face challenges securing their equal rights in the larger society.

Then Ann Erika explained that even though she was born in a very racist area, she was raised with respect for the spiritual life of the Native American. One time, however, her mother took her to a Catholic church to see how they practiced in the church. She told her mother that she liked the Catholic rituals; her mother never took her back to the church, insisting on the observance of their Native American spiritualism. When Ann Erika was seventeen she was talking with her neighbor, telling him that she sees herself as nothing more than a blade of grass. He felt she was putting herself down and got upset, trying to help her realize that this insignificant self-image was not good. But she explained that this humility is intrinsic to Native American spirituality: "Our life on Earth is short and we will leave, just like someone plucking the life from this blade of grass life out of the soil."

These women also spoke about some of the differences among the Native American clans. In some clans, women will keep the spiritual and political treaties while teaching. In other clans women teach, but men write and preserve treaties. When it comes to family lifestyle, some Native Americans can have up to seven wives, but the women own the house. Usually when a mother has a baby she would wait for seven years before giving birth to another baby because she needs seven years to raise each child.

We came to understand how powerful the place of symbolism is in Native American spirituality. One important symbol is the dream catcher, a circle of netting with an empty circle in the center. The netted area is meant to capture and filter out any nightmares during sleep and the empty circle allows only good dreams to remain. Ann Erika was so kind. She gave me a handmade dream catcher made by her cousin. The eagle feather is another important Native American symbol that represents honor and a Native American will receive a feather once he performs an honorable act for his or her community.

These symbols are important because they represent cooperation with the Great Spirit and all the ways this Spirit manifests in life. Paul the healer whose name means "hallow bone" told us stories to understand Ojibwe Ceremonial Practice and how the symbol and the Spirit work together for healing. One day he saw a white light and another day he dreamed of a black pipe; his friend told him that this pipe was a symbol that he could be a special healer in the tribe. Sometime later, his friend James was told that he had a brain illness and that he might die that night. Paul started to smoke the black pipe and pray for his friend and next morning the friend was cured. Another miracle happened when Paul himself had a heart attack and something took his soul to the sky and showed him flashing lights. A voice told him that these are the people praying for you; then the voice took him back to his body. The voice asked Paul to tell this story to everyone. That's why he was sharing his story with us, and now, and out of respect for him, I am documenting it here. Apparently hundreds of people have been

123

cured upon hearing this story though I have yet to meet one. The day ended with all of the Native Americans who were present singing this song:

> *Wehay yahoe haya*
>
> *Jonkolo dalomo*
>
> *Washla hela baya leyo hee*
>
> *Bela tu kashlaya*

. .. .

DAY FIFTY NINE :: MONDAY
NOVEMBER 10, 2008
"Before you contradict an old man, my fair friend, you should endeavor to understand him."
— George Santayana, American philosopher, (1863-1952)

The sessions today were at the Four Winds. Formerly a church, the building is a community center where the people of the land meet as refugees. The host began our sessions for the day by burning incense and touching each of us with an eagle feather that had been dipped in the smoke of this scent. Then they sang the following eagle song:

> *Mea toka hea hapy tu awake yelo hea*
> *Wamble greshka wa yelo hea*
> *aya awa yelo hea*
>
> *The person is coming first*
> *This one is flying first*
> *An eagle is coming*

Today's topic was close to my heart because it was about Canada as the first nation. Canada is my second home because I spent five years earning my Ph.D. at McGill University in Montreal. Sharon Venne, the first speaker today, is so sincere and serious. I know she understands the beauty of her country well even though she does not call it Canada. Native Americans call Canada "the great turtle island." Sharon is so proud of being a Native American that she refuses to be called Canadian, and whenever she is asked where is she from she would say from "the great turtle island."

One of the difficulties Sharon faces in her presentation with us is the use of the English language. In her Native American language there is no masculine or feminine; there is a word for a third person, when he or she is absent, that would be very useful to her in trying to speak to us. The very word that represents her culture has no match in English. Generally speaking English for Sharon has no logic and she asked for our patience as we carried forward the discussion. I was reminded of my previous dialogue with Professor Firestone and began to wonder about just how much can be learned when one actually tries to learn the native language of the person one chooses as a dialogue partner.

The Canadian government tried to take the indigenous people's land and give it to other Canadian people because the land has diamonds and uranium. Sharon works to protect indigenous rights through the Canadian legal system. She studies cases until she finds those that can be used to set the precedence for indigenous rights. The indigenous land is bigger than France and they have its entire map and know when to hunt and mine in different sections, so it was easier for them to make agreements with the government about their land.

In 1992, indigenous Canadians wanted to celebrate the year as it had been five hundred years since Columbus had landed in North America, but the Canadian government refused to make any special designation of the year. Sharon has experienced many other setbacks and misunderstandings due to a lack of recognition and understanding of indigenous issues. After experiencing too many racist moments, she quit her tenured position at the Sacqwachian University in Canada.

But these setbacks related to racism are not isolated to Canada; Sharon was once invited to lecture at the International Institute for Human Rights in Paris. She wanted to speak about the colonizing of indigenous land, but the director of the Institute asked her not to lecture on that topic. When Sharon asked why, he said that she should realize that the issue was closed and that she lived in an era beyond colonization. She knows we have not come so far and said she will continue teaching about colonization.

Another time an institute in NY invited Sharon to come to explain why indigenous women did not sign the Beijing women's rights statement. Sharon was direct to say, "Because we do not agree with what you wrote." She continued explaining that indigenous people have rights by virtue of living on the land, and do not need the UN to give them any rights. International treaties and statements cause more problems for minorities because often the specific situations of the minorities are not taken into consideration. And finally, the international statements are written for humans only and do not show sufficient attention and care about buffalos, moose, deer, bears, fish, and other creatures. Again, the focus of such statements is more often individualistic than communal.

Mohammad Ali asked about elders, when and how would one become an elder among the indigenous people? The answer was that there are different kind of elders: one for history, one for spirituality and so on. One of the Native Americans present said that although she is a great-grandmother, she is not considered an elder because her mother is still alive, so if one of your predecessors is still alive then you cannot yet be an elder.

The elders play a great role in preserving the land, for example the Inuit (i.e., Eskimos) used to live on the ice of the sea about five miles away from the land.

But, the last few years they have had less snow and it is about fifty-seven miles from land which changed their life. It is even snowing later and later every year. It used to start snowing in September, but this year it did not snow until late October as a result of global warming, demonstrating how badly it affects the environment. Another example that demonstrates how Canadians are destroying the environment is that they are the only country in the world that allows dumping toxic waste in pure lakes. Now Alaska is following their lead. Politically and environmentally speaking, America is the worst country in the world when it comes to damaging global ecology. Their nuclear weapon industry, their oil industry, and other heavy industries have the worst influence on our Earth, yet they could not care less, refusing to sign international agreements that protect the environment. Ironically, most states have environmental organizations, and also many universities have departments that offer courses focusing on the environment but when it comes to practice they are lacking, big-time.

At lunch we saw a couple of other practices that honor the elders who have died. To help make them feel happy by being remembered, a piece of food is set aside for them. Also, our Native American friends put four portions of tobacco at the edge of the table because the souls of their ancestors like tobacco. Sometimes, they place the food outside their homes as well.

After lunch Thompson Williams gave a presentation about Caddo people. He posted a picture of fire and told us how he views life through this fire because as long as this fire is alive, then people are alive. He spoke about how fire and words are similar: words bring life, and can be warm or burn. Williams asked about the religions represented in the group. Tink told him there are six Muslims, three Catholics, and one Jew. Williams responded by sharing experiences with Catholics that had scared him: once a Catholic preacher was telling him stories and Williams asked him where had he gotten those stories. The preacher said "from the Bible." They then tried to find them in the Bible and could not; the preacher with confusion said he had always been told they were there. Williams could not respect a storyteller who did not know where his stories originated. Another preacher asked Williams if Native Americans had a Bible. Williams explained how they learn to appreciate life and the Creator from every tree, animal, bird, rain and every living thing around us. The preacher said they then had no actual Bible and Williams puzzled how people would limit themselves to one way of discovering the Creator. His story was about a man who comes to him to tell him that he had lost trust in life and in his faith. Williams talked with him to heal him and when he was done, the man thanked him. He also made a request that their encounter be kept secret as he was the priest at a local Catholic church who was supposed to heal and guide people. His people might lose trust in him if he knew the spiritual solace he had received had come from a Native American.

Towards the end of this session I thanked Williams for his touching lecture and asked him to explain one of his paintings. I think both musicians and artists express many of their thoughts and feelings through their art and I wondered if Williams could speak about them. Kindly, he picked one of his paintings and did articulate its meaning well. The old man in the painting represented the elders who keep Native American traditions from dying; the white and red garment he wore represented the spiritual color white with which they paint their faces in order to communicate with the spirit of their ancestors and red represented power. That's why they wear red color on their hearts when they dance but wear a blue color on their hearts, representing calmness, when they pray. There is a yellow scarf around the man's neck. The yellow represents his tribe, and the way he ties the scarf shows that he is a healer (as people wear different signs to represent their roles). A few horses stood in the back of the picture all facing the same direction. He explained how the horses are in the back of the picture to show children especially that the pictures speak of history. They are standing in the same direction to indicate the future and the importance of history for the future. Again, his explanation demonstrated the great importance symbols hold in Native Americans' way of life.

Knowing that about 80% of Native American men at one time or another have been incarcerated in American prisons and, that of that number, 80% are there for offences related to alcohol, Williams thinks that having Native Americans in prison prevents them from having more children, which is one other road to genocide. I asked Williams why he thought these problems exist, and how they are trying to solve them. He explained that part of the problem is that Native Americans think it is manly to drink and another part is that they want to escape their miserable life. This issue is one of the most serious problems of Native Americans.

In the afternoon Sharon, Paul, Glenn and Tink spoke to us about Rite of Vigil ceremonies. In this session, the presenters shared with us some of their personal spiritual experiences.

Paul told us that one day he was walking and a voice told him to look up. When he looked up he saw four eagles flying in the four cardinal directions. He was then taken to the sky where the sky and the stars started to move, creating a hole through which energy came to him. He was given special knowledge and he asked what these teachings were for. The voice told him that he would know when the time comes.

Sharon preferred to tell us about how Cree women preserve spirituality rather than speak of her own experience. In the sun dance they fast for four days and dance all day, sweating while fasting. When they are sweating, they should be covering even their hair and faces so no one will know who they are in this state. Women should not get involved in the dance until they are ready for it because they are putting their soul in the hand of the spiritual soul. During these four days, women are allowed to have one meal. One of the ceremonies at this time recognizes a girl's passage into puberty. She receives a new name and fasts from sunrise to sunset. Then the women share in a festival with her, explaining to the girl what it is to be a woman.

Glenn who lectured yesterday about the indigenous political system today spoke about his own spirituality. As he did, he wept, saying this was the first time he had ever shared his spiritual life in front of non-Native Americans. Glenn was born in the Shawnee tribe but he was raised with the Lakota tribe. Their spirituality does not require a choice to have faith, as the missionaries suggested, because this way of living with faith is empirical, immediate, and does not need intersession like Christians who need priests. Glenn can speak to his ancestors directly, but he never talks to bears as Hollywood shows depict Native Americans talking to animals. The most influential experience he had was during the sun dance, when he danced for four days and he gave part of his flesh and blood, and stuck a piece of bone or tree into his body. Once he was hanged on the tree one meter above the ground and he felt no pain. Then he felt his ancestor come and ask him if he wanted to go with them, which would mean that he would die. So he started to think about them, and his father who passed away. While he was thinking, other Native Americans pulled him down to the ground. He asked them why they pulled him down, and they said we did not want you or anyone to die here because the government will prevent us from having our sun dance. He receives wisdom from the ancestors and has learned how not to fear death and to appreciate life from his experiences of the sun dance.

. . ..

DAY SIXTY: TUESDAY
NOVEMBER 11, 2008
"These people are very unskilled in arms...with 50 men they could all be subjected and made to do all that one wished."

— Christopher Columbus, America adventurer, (1451-1506)

Tink Tinker decided today to tell us about himself and some of his work. Tink talks about the notion of God and Creator, and how Native Americans sometimes use the word Creator to refer to God and sometimes they use it to refer to the Creator which is the Spirit. Tink quoted Albert Whitehat from the Lakota who said Christians have a God and Native Americans have no God; they have een (stone), all of life. The entire world comes from een. In the beginning was een, i.e., he is comparatively referring to the first verse in the Bible "in the beginning it was the word." One day a Native American was talking in front of over four hundred missionaries and asked them to describe God. They replied to him that no one knows what God looks like. So he took a stone and said what if I say this stone is God; how would you prove me wrong? They were speechless. He went on to challenge them saying that he, of course, does not believe in this stone as God, but he wanted to make the point that no one can prove anyone wrong about their belief in God if no one can describe God. There are many sacred natural powers that all Native Americans believe in, such as the sun, the stones, the fire, the eagle, and the buffalo. Sometimes, based on regional differences, one sacred natural element is praised more than another. In Mexico, for example, there are no eagles but another type of bird would hold a place of reverence in a ceremony.

Tink is writing a book on Native American theology, because he finds it important to write about his own theology rather than have it categorized with Semitic religions. One of Tink's explanations of his theology is that Native Americans do not worship stones as idols. I told him that in the Quran, God describes beliefs that different groups of people have. He describes one group that worships stones. I had thought of such worship as making an idol of the stone. But, after listening to these Native Americans, I understand better how worship of stones could mean worship of their essence as created by God. Tink concurred, confirming that he does not worship the stones for themselves, but he knows that these stones have energy that guides him and comes to him whenever he needs. He reached into his pocket to pull out three such stones: one kept in leather and two other stones representing the eagle.

After a nice shopping break at a Native American store, we had lunch then started the second session, which was a panel on healing ceremonies presented by Tink, Sharon, Paul, and Thompson Williams. Sharon is from the Cree tribe which is a bear clan. This clan is famous for medicine because as a bear they walk on Earth and pick up herbs and use them to heal people. Sharon's grandmother was a gifted healing person from whom she learned. Sharon's brother-in-law is from a buffalo clan, and when he was sick and hospitalized, she visited him. And when she brought food to him, she would not bring buffalo because he does not eat it as it is the symbol of his clan.

Watching robins come in the spring was enjoyable, especially listening to them sing. Mother robins reminded us of our mothers, but robins also served another purpose. If you hear a robin cry, you have to watch out as it is believed to be a bad omen. Then one of them told this story:

> *"I was ten or eleven years old and staying at my grandfather's house along the Minnesota-Canadian border. It was a summer day; one of those slow summer days. I was enjoying watching people walk by. I saw this girl (whom I later fell madly in love with when I was in high school). She walked right over. I tried to look handsome. She sat down on the grass with me. My heart was full of joy and excitement. I could actually hear the constructions of poetry in my mind and feel in my heart what would shape my wisdom for generations to come. Then I heard the robin sing. Except, the robin didn't cry but brought disaster. He pooped without warning on my head and it ran down on my face. I was pretty adept at getting through most situations. But this was an exception. This girl of my dreams broke into laughter. In the meantime, I was trying to wipe it off my head. I would never forgive that robin for not giving me warning. If this had been you, you too, would have been affected by it. Your blood pressure would drop, but depression wouldn't weigh you down. Even if you were to suffer from cancer, laughter would help your body to recuperate*

and generate the proper hormones to heal. Our elders had this wisdom. So a big part of healing is knowing how to clown around. You've really got to know how to make people laugh. But, because we are pathetic two-legged creatures, there will be times we will do something wrong and have to eat humble pie.

One of the roles of the healer is to allow others to learn how something that has been done wrong can be restorative. Native Americans understand this kind of healing wisdom. For example, my most deadly audience was Lutheran church women. I could tell jokes, seemingly exciting news, but not a single change in the mood of the room. I would usually like to get some feedback. Afterwards there is always coffee, and I like to go from table to table and find out how they found my presentation. The had liked the humor. There is healing in a presence in which you help others to learn how they can use humor for healing in different situations."

The essential core for Native American philosophy is healing because it maintains balance, even if they end the life of an ear of corn in order to eat it, they take its life for balance and they also give life to corn to maintain balance. But when they take the life of a corn, they need to be healed from taking that life. The elders decide who the healer in each clan is as well as assign the clan affiliation to newborn babies. Native Americans do not marry from the same clan for two reasons; one is genetic, to maintain healthier generations, and second to avoid any possible problems between the close families and clans in case the marriage does not go well. They also avoid delineating words like step-mother, or half-brother or sister-in-law etc. The loyalty of a Native American will be to his clan, not to his family. Each clan is known for its spritual gift: the bear clan as mentioned earlier, is known for carrying medicine, the eagle clan is known for being visionaries, the buffalo clan is known for being leaders, and the beaver clan is known for construction. One day a young Native American wanted to know the best among the clans, so the elders told him that no one is better than the other because life is based on balance and each clan needs the others and each clan has something to offer to the others.

Towards the end of the day and just before the reception with Illif faculty members, Professor Wasey thanked the program organizer, stating that he would make a confession in front of two Catholic priests, Michael and Serge, that we had been half bright until we met the Native American then we became full bright (i.e., Fulbright). The group members did know the Semitic religions and eastern cultures, but we did not know about native culture and spirituality until we experienced it with a great group of Native Americans representing different clans. I must state here that the strength of the United States of America comes from being open and honest with their people. Although Native Americans in general do not appreciate the American government or Christianity, the religion of the majority of Americans, the State Department arranged this program for Fulbright scholars who come from different countries and backgrounds to meet and discuss the spiritual thoughts, social views and political positions of these natives.

. . ..

DAY SIXTY ONE :: WEDNESDAY
NOVEMBER 12, 2008
"One man can be a crucial ingredient on a team, but one man cannot make a team."
— Kareem Abdul-Jabbar, American athlete, (1947-)

We took a tour trip to downtown Denver, and it has its uniqueness just like any other American city. There were two main universities in the city, and we passed by the football stadium.

Football is the most popular American sport and is not what most of the world calls football (e.g., soccer in America). Rather than kicking a round ball, an elliptical football is caught and carried. Rather than quick players wearing only shin protection, football favors bulky players covering their heads, arms, and bodies with thick padding. Finally, rather than being constant and improvisational, the action in football is frequently broken up as each team develops and acts on strategies.

In football, two teams of eleven players take either the offensive or the defensive side. The offense tries to carry the ball through the defense to the far end of the field, called the end zone. The defense tries to prevent them from reaching the end zone either by catching one of their passes or by grabbing the player with the ball and dragging him to the ground. The offense either sends players to prevent defenders from reaching the ball-carrier, or they send people that can catch the ball if the carrier becomes surrounded. Teams get six points if they reach the end zone, plus one or two points for various other actions after reaching the end zone. If the offense scores, or if the defense takes the ball, then the defense becomes the offense. The game is officially an hour long, but the clock is stopped during strategy sessions, so it generally ends up lasting three or four hours. When time runs out, the team that has earned the most points wins.

Football season in America runs from the end of summer to mid-winter. Organized football is played in high school, college, and professionally on a national level. Many small towns, especially in the South, are very proud of their high school teams. Some colleges use the sport to make money, and offer large scholarships to talented high-school players to come play for their teams. Most large cities have teams that play on the national level. Thirty-two teams are broken into two conferences with four divisions each. Each division's teams play each other and advance in rank according to how many times they have won, and how strong the teams they defeated were. Six teams from each conference play, then compete in a national tournament. Finally, the two best teams play in the Super Bowl to decide the national winner.

The Super Bowl, which happens in early February, is a colossal cultural event. Even people who do not care about football, or sports in general, or even understand the basic rules, will watch the Super Bowl. Families, churches, local governments, and bars

131

will hold large parties for people to watch the game, eat snacks, and drink beer. Because the Super Bowl is so popular, companies will spend several million dollars to develop very elaborate commercials to show during the game. Some people prefer watching the commercials over the game itself. The Super Bowl is usually played on a Sunday, so watching it does not require time off from work, but even people who work the following day will party long after the game is finished, well into the morning, lamenting their defeat or celebrating their victory.

Football is not the only famous sport; basketball is also another popular game. Basketball was invented by Canadian professor James Naismith who was looking for a game to play during the winter of 1891 when it was too cold to go outside. He eventually ended up nailing a peach basket to the wall of the gymnasium. The bottom of the basket was removed sometime later.

Basketball is played by two teams consisting of five people, wearing light jerseys and shorts. A large, rubber ball must be bounced, or dribbled, on the floor while a player moves, trying to get to the opposite side of the playing court. The other team tries to take the ball, either by interfering with the holder's dribbling or by catching the ball when it's thrown to another player. At the end of the court, the basket, a metal hoop with a net hung on it, is fixed on a plexiglass backboard, which is either hung from the ceiling or raised on a pole. If the player evades the defense, he or she must put the ball through the top of the hoop, usually by bouncing off the backboard, but practiced players can arc the ball through the hoop, and some can simply jump high enough to shove the ball in. The opposition tries to interfere with all of these plays, and, if they get the ball, immediately begin taking it back across the court to the other team's basket. If a player scores, the team gets two points or three if they score by pitching the ball from twenty feet away.

Basketball is played in high school, college, and nationally. There are thirty teams in the National Basketball Association, divided into two fifteen-team conferences with three regions. The season is divided into two parts, the regular season, where each team plays all of the other teams at least once, and the playoffs, where the winners from each region, plus the five teams from each conference with the best records, play against each other. The winner is decided in a best-of-seven tournament that usually ends in March.

The greatest American basketball player was Michael Jordan of the Chicago Bulls. Jordan excelled at every aspect of the game, both defense and offense, but is most famous for his incredible jumping ability. He could repeatedly jump high enough to slam the ball through the hoop, and could reach the basket from so far that it seemed like he was flying. Jordan was a stand-out player who significantly enhanced the popularity of basketball both in America and abroad. Players at home and abroad aspire to be his successor. In fact, many of the new stars in basketball are recruited from other countries by American teams, such as Chinese Yao Ming, who at 7'6" is currently the NBA's tallest player.

. . . .

DAY SIXTY TWO :: THURSDAY
NOVEMBER 13, 2008
"Our life is frittered away by detail ... simplify, simplify."
— Henry David Thoreau, American Philosopher and Poet, (1817-1862)

Americans are easy to read and befriend. On my way back to Chicago, a young nice-looking lady was sitting next to me in the airplane. I asked her whether she was from Denver visiting Chicago or the other way around. She smiled as she replied that she was not from or traveling to either city. She went on to explain that she lived and studied in California, but that her grandparents live in Chicago, and she visits them once or twice a year. I asked her how she spends her time in Chicago when visiting them. She said that she just likes to spend time with her grandparents and sometimes she babysits for their neighbor while she is there. She went on to tell me about her grandparents' health and how she takes care of their medication. The conversation continued as she told me about her school and friends. I don't think her case is special, but rather she was like most of the Americans I met, easygoing people who don't mind sharing general information about their lives with others.

On the other hand, this generalization only goes so far. Individualism is one of the strongest character traits in most of Americans I met. Although Roosevelt succeeded in helping America break free somewhat from its isolation, there is still an unseen barrier Americans build around themselves. When I first came to the U.S., it took me a few months to invite my American neighbor over for a party in my home. It was a couple more months before he invited me to watch the Super Bowl with his family and friends in his home. We did become friends, and after I left the U.S. we stayed in touch.

Chapter 7

"*Non-violence leads to the highest ethics, which is the goal of all evolution. Until we stop harming all other living beings, we are still savages.*"

Thomas Edison, AMERICAN SCIENTIST, (1847-1931)

. . . .

DAY SIXTY THREE :: FRIDAY
NOVEMBER 14, 2008
"Do what's right for you, as long as it don't hurt no one."
— Elvis Presley, American singer, (1935-1977)

There was a gathering for the Fulbrighters in Chicago and the surrounding areas, where I met several exchange students, assistant teachers, and researchers. The Fulbrighters in that small gathering were from all over the world, and after the program, a few of us decided to stay in Chicago for couple of days. One of them was an assistant teacher from Germany who was teaching Dutch at a college in suburban Chicago. We went out for lunch and had to go to three different restaurants before finding one that served vegan meals. Vegans are stricter than vegetarians. Vegans do not eat animal or even products of animal, like eggs and milk; I really do not know how they manage. Unlike in my conversation with Americans as exemplified with the young woman visiting her grandparents, the conversation I had with this German colleague was limited to the Fulbright program we shared in common.

135

. . . .

DAY SIXTY FOUR :: SATURDAY
NOVEMBER 15, 2008
"I know not what others may choose but, as for me, give me liberty, or give me death!"
— Patrick Henry, American Patriot, Symbol for American struggle for liberty, (1736-1799)

. . . .

DAY SIXTY FIVE :: SUNDAY
NOVEMBER 16, 2008
"Lead, follow, or get out of the way."
— Thomas Paine, American Writer, (1737-1809)

Back in Chicago, I was happy to meet with Dennis Martin again. He took me to the Latin church in Chicago. With between 225 and 300 million adherents worldwide, the Eastern Orthodox Church is the second largest Christian denomination in the world. Its churches are united by their common theological beliefs, but each congregation also maintains a certain amount of autonomy because each region is "autocephalous," meaning that the bishop who oversees the region within which the local church exists does not report to a higher-ranking bishop.

In the first few centuries of its existence, Christianity spread across the Greco-Roman

world, both east and west of the Mediterranean Sea. The Eastern segment of this movement, situated in the Hellenized, or Greek-cultured, portion of the Roman Empire, laid the earliest foundations of Eastern Orthodoxy. Whereas Western, Latin Christians claimed Rome as their center for theological leadership, those in the East claimed Constantinople (Istanbul).

During these developmental years for Christianity, disagreements were not infrequent. Questions arose quickly such as: Is Jesus a man or God? Is God three or one? Did Jesus have one will, a human one, or two, both God and human? Christian leaders did not always agree on the answers to these questions. Thus, in response to disagreement, theological meetings would be held to draw Christians together. These meetings were called "ecumenical councils." Eastern Orthodox Christians claim that the first seven of these meetings (from 325 CE to 787 CE) represent their own beliefs.

Among the important beliefs represented by these first seven councils are the fact that God is three persons in one essence, that Jesus is both fully God and fully human, that Mary is the birth mother of God (*theotokos* in the Greek), that the Holy Spirit is fully divine, and that icons (artistic representations of biblical characters and events) can function as aids to worship but should not be worshipped themselves.

In the year 1054, Eastern Orthodox and Roman Catholic Christians split definitively. Michael Cerulari, the leading Christian in Constantinople, would not recognize the claim to universal authority being made by the church in Rome. Both church leaders (Pope Leo IX in Rome and Cerulari in Constantinople) claimed that the other was significantly wrong theologically and, therefore, should not be considered a part of the "true church." Among the more significant theological reasons for this split was the claim of the Eastern Orthodox

*"Baptism" is an ancient religious practice, rooted in Jewish ritual, in which
the baptized person is ceremonially cleansed. Today among Christians this
ancient ritual is preserved as a Christian initiatory rite.*

Church that the Holy Spirit proceeds only from the Father and not from the Father and the
Son. After the collapse of the Byzantine Empire under the Ottomans, Eastern Orthodoxy
moved eastward, eventually finding a strong presence as far east as Moscow.

The historical theologians who have made the most impact on Eastern Orthodoxy are
Origen of Alexandria (185-254), the 4th Century Cappadocian Fathers: Basil of Caesarea,
Gregory of Nyssa, and Gregory of Nanzianzus, and Gregory Palamas (1296-1359).
Vladimir Lossky (1903-1958) was an influential Orthodox theologian of the 20th Century.

. . ..

DAY SIXTY SIX :: MONDAY
November 17, 2008

*"Don't be trapped by dogma, which is living with the results of other people's thinking…
and most important, have the courage to follow your heart and intuition. They somehow
already know what you truly want to become. Everything else is secondary."*

— Steve Jobs, American entrepreneur, (1955-)

Today I learned about American Southern Baptists, who represent the largest
Protestant Christian denomination, with over 16 million members and
42,000 churches nationwide, the majority of which exist in the South. Other
Baptist denominations include the Northern Baptists, General Baptists, and Regular
Baptists. The issues of slavery and the rights of the southern United States have been
acknowledged by historians as the top reasons why the Southern Baptist Convention
separated from its northern counterparts in 1845; in 1995 the Southern Baptist
Convention issued a formal apology, acknowledging this unfortunate aspect of its origin.

"Baptism" is an ancient religious practice, rooted in Jewish ritual, in which the
baptized person is ceremonially cleansed. In Greek the word *baptizo* means simply
"to dip" or "to wash." Today among Christians this ancient ritual is preserved as a
Christian initiatory rite. It represents the cleansing that a person is said to receive upon
conversion and is, therefore, a symbol of the miraculous work that God has performed
on the person's behalf. Its historical origin as a Christian rite can be found in the book
of Acts in the New Testament. There, as happened for example between Philip and the
Ethiopian Eunuch, those who were converted to Christianity were baptized in order to
signify their inclusion in the church.

As is suggested by their name, American churches associated with the Baptist movement
today stress the importance of this ritual in a person's conversion to Christianity. Whereas
all Christian denominations hold up baptism as an important Christian ceremony, only
Baptist Christians reserve it solely for those who are converted volitionally, for those adults
who make a decision to join Christianity. In other Christian denominations, baptism

may be administered to infants, whose entrance into the Christian family is decided by their parents. Yet for Baptists, whose theology is rooted in a robust appreciation for the individual, the act of baptism is reserved only for those who are old enough to decide for themselves that they desire to commit to Christianity.

Most Baptist Christians perform this rite of initiation by following an ornate ceremony. A pastor and the convert will wade into water that is waist-deep, often wearing white robes that symbolize the cleansing that has taken place through God's forgiveness. The pastor will hold up one hand, reciting a formula in which the baptized person is named followed by: "I baptize you in the name of the Father, and of the Son, and of the Holy Spirit." After this invocation, the pastor lowers the person fully into the water and then raises him or her back up.

Baptism functions as a unique theological symbol in which the new Christian is able to physically experience the new spiritual benefits. It symbolizes the clean heart that Christians trust is theirs upon the forgiveness of their sins. It symbolizes the changed life that Christians hope to adopt upon conversion, and it symbolizes the death and resurrection of Jesus, which Christians believe provides the power through which they are able to live lives committed to God.

The history of Baptist origins is a much debated topic. Among non-Baptist historians, the general consensus is that the movement originated both out of the 16th Century Anabaptist movement in Switzerland and the 17th Century Puritan movement in England. The earliest Baptists were moved by their careful study of the Bible and adherence to the practices of the earliest church. They saw in the church, founded and led by Jesus' apostles, the purest form of Christian community, untainted by centuries of speculative dogma imposed by ecclesial authorities. Thus, they prioritized issues like church-state separation, personal discipleship (i.e., following Jesus), and the practice of baptizing only adult believers who had expressly stated their desire to commit their lives to Jesus.

In America this teaching was represented by some of the earliest colonists of New England: Roger Williams (1600-1695) and John Clarke (1609-1676), whose churches were founded on the separatist foundations rooted in the European radical reformation. Henry Dunster (1612-1659), the first president of Harvard University in Boston, was also a Baptist, preaching against infant baptism and eventually deciding not to baptize his fourth child as an infant.

A common theme among all of the earliest Baptists was their experience of persecution, even from other Protestants. The Lutheran and Calvinist churches of Europe, and to some extent in colonial America, saw the Baptist reformers as a threat to the fabric of Christian society, in which church and state were harmoniously united. They gave them the titles "Anabaptists" (or "again-baptists") and "Baptists" as pejorative titles that eventually were used to respectfully refer to these groups. Ironically, as a form of persecution, many of the earliest Baptists were drowned, sadistically symbolizing their practice of water baptism.

138

DAY SIXTY SEVEN :: TUESDAY
NOVEMBER 18, 2008
"And so, my fellow Americans, ask not what your country can do for you; ask what you can do for your country."

— John F. Kennedy, 35th American President, (1917-1963)

My meeting today with Loyola Provost and Vice-Rector for International Students was kind of a complementary one. I paid them a visit to thank them for being a great host and to inform them of the programs and lectures I am involved in at Loyola. The conversation went on to discuss the Saudi students at Loyola and in the U.S. in general. The most common issue for Saudi students is getting accepted at an American university. Two years ago, King Abdullah of Saudi Arabia provided about eighty-thousand scholarships for Saudi students to study abroad, and about half of them would go to the U.S., but they have to be accepted at a university in order to get the scholarship. This scholarship program will influence Saudi Arabia at all levels. Compared to the scholarship programs that Saudi had in the '70s, the influence they had in changing and developing Saudi Arabia will be doubled. The flood of Saudi students who will be coming back to Saudi Arabia from different countries will have a strong effect, but we have to be cautious as they may return with things that are good or bad for our society.

Unfortunately, many of the Saudi students in the U.S. are young and are taken by the surface of American culture. They miscomprehend the true meaning of freedom, modernity, etc. As a Saudi student must attend preparatory workshops before they go abroad, I think they should also attend rehab workshops when they come back, otherwise they will find it very difficult to settle in our strict society after being in an open country, or they will break the rules. Both scenarios are not good outcomes.

DAY SIXTY EIGHT :: WEDNESDAY
NOVEMBER 19, 2008
"Writing is an exploration. You start from nothing and learn as you go."

— E. L. Doctorow, American author, (1931-)

This evening William Scott and I presented a panel on "Muslim-Christian Relations: Current Challenges and Possibilities." The panel discussed the relationship between Islam and Christianity in different eras. We began our panel with the pre-Islamic era and the story of Bahira, who was a Christian religious scholar. This was followed by the rise of Islam era and the example provided was

Waraqa, a Christian religious practitioner. We then discussed the early Islamic period with the story of Najashi, a Christian political leader. Next, the peak of Islamic history, with a discussion about Hercules, another Christian political leader. Afterwards, we discussed the righteous caliph Abu Bakr, and his positive positions with Christianity based on the Quranic verses about dialogue. We concluded with the current official religious leaders' position and political activities, including King Abdullah of Saudi Arabia; three interfaith conferences and initiatives; Mecca Declaration (June, 2008), Madrid Declaration, World Conference on Dialogue (July, 2008), and New York Initiative (November, 2008).

Later on in the evening, while I was going to the café where I usually write, I bumped into a student at Loyola who converted from Hinduism to Islam. She reminded me of a student from the Theology Department who is half Persian and half Mexican. They both have mixed religious and cultural backgrounds.

. .. .

DAY SIXTY NINE :: THURSDAY
NOVEMBER 20, 2008
"Non-violence leads to the highest ethics, which is the goal of all evolution. Until we stop harming all other living beings, we are still savages."
— Thomas Edison, American scientist, (1847-1931)

Many Americans stand up for causes and support them voluntarily. Dr. Kristen Stilt, a professor of Law, is a perfect example of someone who spends lots of time and effort working for a good cause. Kristin cares about animal rights, especially dogs. Besides her own dog, she is taking care of many stray dogs by volunteering at a shelter in Chicago. She went further to get involved in establishing shelters for dogs in Egypt while travelling to participate in a conference there. From a very general topic, such as the environment, to specific areas of interest, you will find thousands of local and national organizations in America.

Once I opened the yellow pages, and searched for environmental non-profit organizations. I called a few of them to ask them how to set up and develop a similar organization in Saudi Arabia. Surprisingly, more than half of them were ready to come and meet with me voluntarily, and bring me materials and guidelines on how to establish and run such organization. Although I have the material and willingness to volunteer to establish an organization, it is not as easy to register and run a non-profit organization in Saudi Arabia as it is in the U.S.

Many people in Saudi Arabia, like America, love to volunteer for good causes. However, volunteering work is somewhat restricted to religious organizations which were badly affected after 9-11. To a certain extent, it is better to revamp volunteerism in Saudi

Arabia. Volunteers need to be trained and non-profit organizations must be reevaluated. The whole process should be easier than it is now.

. . ..

DAY SEVENTY :: FRIDAY
NOVEMBER 21, 2008
"Keep away from people who try to belittle your ambitions. Small people always do that, but the really great ones make you feel that you too, can become great."
— Mark Twain, American writer, (1835-1910)

I n all my conversations about Christianity I began to realize just how many different important figures there were. One of the most influential leaders after Jesus was Paul. Christianity grew by leaps and bounds in the Mediterranean during the years following Jesus' death. This exponential growth and the new teachings associated with Christianity were upsetting to some religious leaders of the day. One of these leaders, a Roman citizen by birth and a man trained in the laws of Judaism, was named Saul of Tarsus later to be called Paul as we shall see.

141

Saul was zealous for the protection of Judaism and eventually led a movement of persecution against Christians. The Gospel author, Luke, recorded much of Saul's life in his book "The Acts of the Apostles" in the New Testament. He captured the zeal of Saul's hatred for this movement by saying Saul "breathed out murderous threats" against Christians (Acts 9-1) in a campaign to destroy the church. Yet at the height of this campaign, Saul had a life-changing experience. According to Luke, Saul was traveling to the Palestinian city of Damascus, when he was blinded by a bright light and knocked from his horse. During this vision Saul conversed with the risen Jesus, and his zeal for destroying the church was transformed into a zeal for promoting it.

Saul took up the Latin name "Paul," signifying his conversion to Christianity and his commitment to non-Jew converts. It is by this name that he is remembered among Christians today. Paul spent a number of years traveling around the Mediterranean, preaching that Jesus was the Son of God and that peace with God could be found only through the life, death, and resurrection of Jesus. During his travels Paul corresponded with new converts by writing letters. Today, these letters make up an important part of the Christian scriptures. Islamic sources attribute the introduction of new concepts to Christianity not taught by Jesus, such as the trinity, to Paul.

Aside from the Apostle Paul, perhaps no other Christian thinker has been as influential as Augustine (354 - 430 CE), the North African Bishop from Hippo Regis. He lived during a time when Christianity was still attempting to find its voice. Augustine's sharp mind, winsome preaching, and voluminous writings were of vital importance in refining a number of Christian doctrines. His life began under the care of his mother, Monica, whose devotion to Christ would have long-lasting impact on her son. Although Augustine gave up his mother's religion during his younger years, he eventually returned to the Christianity that she so dutifully followed.

The story of Augustine's life is recorded by him in a book entitled *Confessions*. Considered the first autobiography of Western literature, Augustine's *Confessions* is addressed to God and written as a prayer. Augustine invites the reader to listen in on his most intimate thoughts, as he recalls his life from infancy to adulthood, praising God for the way order had been established from his life of disorder.

Like any of history's most influential thinkers, Augustine's career was marked with controversy. His own theology was developed as a philosophical reflection on Christian scripture but also in response to a number of movements whose teachings he saw as dangerous to the fundamental concepts of Christianity. Primarily, there were four historical movements to which Augustine responded: Manichaeism, Arianism, Pelagianism, and Donatism.

In response to the "problem of evil," which questioned how God could be both good and all-powerful, while evil existed in the world, the Manicheans taught that evil is distinct from God, that it is an eternal substance existing always in contrast to God. In response to this teaching, Augustine taught that evil is not derived from God, since God can only create good things. But he also maintained that evil does exist. In order to account for this paradox, Augustine asserted that evil is nothing more than a "privation of the good," that it can only exist where goodness does not, and that in and of itself it has no existence. Many Muslim philosophers adopted this explanation of evil, and conclude that God did not create evil.

Arianism was a Christian movement of the 3rd Century CE that tried to maintain the radical unity of God. In response to the trinitarian theology of early Christianity, according to which God is three-in-one, Arians insisted that God could not be three; maintaining such a doctrinal claim would necessitate a polytheistic undercurrent within Christianity. Thus, Arius and his proponents challenged the eternal nature of the Son and the Holy Spirit, the second and third members of the trinity. They held that "there was a time when the son was not" and that he was, therefore, created. In contrast to these claims, Augustine worked carefully through the Christian doctrine of trinity, trying to show its validity as a philosophical claim. He pointed out a number of "trinities" within creation. He stated, for example, that the idea of love is tripartite: it requires a lover, a beloved, and love itself. Arianism was mentioned in Prophet Muhammad's, peace be upon him, letter to Heraclius, stating that if he converted to Islam then he would be rewarded for his conversion and the conversion of all Christians who follow him, but if he decided not to convert to Islam then he should leave the followers of Arius alone or else he would be committing a gross sin. This incident was not clear to Muslim commentators who tried to explain

Muhammad's letter, and they thought Arianism referred to laypersons.

Pelagianism formed the most preoccupying controversy that Augustine faced. According to Pelagius, human nature was created in such a way that God's grace was not needed in order for humans to live righteously and, therefore, to earn salvation. God gave humans a free will; therefore, we must assume that humans have the capacity to live lives completely in harmony with what God would want. Augustine saw in this claim a latent pride, which would minimize the importance of God's grace. He read in Christian scripture that everything given to humans comes from God, which he assumed must include the ability to live a life worthy of God's approval. Even the very ability to please God must come from God. Augustine's encounter with Pelagianism reinforced his appreciation of God's grace. Similar arguments and understandings could be found in Islamic mysticism. Augustine's philosophical background is broadly Neoplatonist, represented by the 3rd Century Platonic philosopher Plotinus. Using this system as the matrix through which he considered the teachings of the scriptures, Augustine presented Christianity as a philosophically viable system. In his lengthy work, *The City of God*, Augustine responded to common critiques against Christianity during the early 5th Century.

And finally, the early portion of the second millennium (11th-13th Centuries) was of major importance for the development of Christian theology. In Western Europe, where Christianity had found a significant foothold, the educational system was shifting, and with it shifted the method of Christian thinking. This came in the form of a movement known as scholasticism, a method of teaching and studying that attempted to answer questions of truth by a variety of methods: question-and-answer, dialectical analysis, commentary on authoritative texts, etc. During this movement, no philosophical stone was left unturned in the thinker's attempt to arrive at the "first principles," or irreducible axioms that form the philosophical foundations on which ideas are based. This shift in epistemology was accompanied by a revival of the study of Aristotle, the Greek philosopher, whose work was both derived from and was a complement to the philosophy of Plato. As these developments were occurring, a differentiation was being made between philosophy and theology, one that had not been made before to the same extent.

Thomas Aquinas, the third major figure in Christianity (1225-1274 CE), entered this epistemological scene equipped with a deep knowledge of Aristotelian logic, of the writings of the church fathers, and of the Hebrew and Christian testaments. His theological project, one that eventually became as influential as any theologian who had gone before him, was an attempt to interweave theology and philosophy. He encouraged the human mind to think theologically, or in relation to its end or purpose. In doing so, Aquinas developed a philosophically technical account of God as the first cause of everything that exists and the final goal of all things. He constructed a "divine science" through which humans can contemplate the "divine cause."

The primary work written by Thomas Aquinas is entitled the *Summa Theologica*, which means broadly "theological summary" or "theological treatise." This unfinished work, which was intended as an introduction to the Christian faith, is divided into three major sections: (1) On God and language about God; (2) On the movement of rational creatures to God; (3) On Jesus, who is the means by which humans and God can meet. Following the scholastic methodology of his time, Aquinas presented his theses by asking and answering questions: "How can we speak of God?" "How does Jesus communicate with God?" "To what degree can humans know God?" In order to answer large questions, Aquinas asks more specific questions, attempting to differentiate within any given subject its first principles. Then Aquinas would address several objections to the questions he raised in order to wrap up satisfying answers.

Among the many important theological moves Aquinas made was his use of the Aristotelian distinction between essence and existence, or "what" something is in contrast to "that" it is. Based on Aquinas' writing, we can speak of God inasmuch as human language can speak of God, which is always imperfect but never pointless.

. . ..

DAY SEVENTY ONE :: SATURDAY
NOVEMBER 22, 2008
"Labor is prior to, and independent of, capital. Capital is only the fruit of labor, and could never have existed if labor had not first existed. Labor is the superior of capital, and deserves much the higher consideration."
— Abraham Lincoln, 16th American President, (1809-1865)

Volunteer efforts are major activities in American neighborhoods. Today I got up early to visit the Midwest Workers Association (MWA) that has sister associations all over America. MWA is an all-volunteer membership organization established in 1996 and funded by the communities from all over Chicago to help provide work for people who have lost their jobs. Out of a city population of two-million, eight-hundred-thousand, about seventy-thousand people in Chicago have lost their jobs.

The first worker association of this kind was established in 1972. MWA is a labor workers' union of a different type. Most of its members can not join labor unions because of the type of jobs they have had. They assist the elderly in their homes, or work in part-time jobs where they do not have any benefits or healthcare. They also assist people in finding health insurance or getting free medical appointments with volunteer doctors. They help finding clothing and pay heating bills for those in need. They give out turkeys and food for Thanksgiving; then toys and food at Christmas.

Every Saturday, MWA members arrange canvasses in groups of two or three. Between four to twenty members go from door-to-door to register more members and introduce the organization's programs and benefits to them. A one-year membership costs sixty-two cents a month; less than eight dollars a year. This Saturday there were ten volunteers and I joined them to help the poor neighbors at Angelwood. Many homes were abandoned because people could not afford to pay their rent or taxes and thus were forced into foreclosure. Luckily, my partner was born in that neighborhood and had lived there since he was young. He told us how busy these empty streets used to be in the '70s and '80s but now no businesses were left.

The canvass was from 11 a.m. until 2 p.m., and we came back to the MWA office to summarize our reports. Our goal is to have thirteen new members, including four members to join us next Saturday for canvassing, and four to join in for the Thursday Thanksgiving program. We reached the numbers we planned and I was able to register two of the thirteen new members. Lunch was canned soup and cake, followed by an hour of discussion about the community situation.

145

. .. .

DAY SEVENTY TWO :: SUNDAY
NOVEMBER 23, 2008
"The American Revolution was a beginning, not a consummation."
— Woodrow Wilson, 28th American President, (1856-1924).

I visited the medieval show in Ohio, and it was not fun at all, but it could be fun for kids. It reminded me of American history. Although I won't go back all the way to discuss the medieval period, I will go back to the early 19th Century during the famous American Civil War.

Ever since the foundation of the United States, slavery had been an institution in the South. Africans were originally purchased from slave traders, and eventually the South began breeding their own. Africans were forced to work at large farms called plantations with no compensation, many under cruel and abusive masters. Harriet Beecher Stowe (1811-1896) described the immorality of slavery in her 1852 novel *Uncle Tom's Cabin*, of which I read a translated version in Arabic when I was in high school. The vivid descriptions of slavery in the book inspired anti-slavery groups that had been becoming more active in the North, calling for an end to the practice. The South angrily resisted Stowe's characterization as exaggerated, but the novel's huge impact defined what slavery meant for many Northerners, and helped entrench the mutual resentments that lead to the Civil War.

The Southern states relied heavily on slavery to produce their major crops — cotton, tobacco, etc. — all of which required a large amount of human labor. Their primarily agricultural economic base was also precarious; the Southern states were generally much poorer than the North. The South wanted to extend the slavery system

throughout the United States, or to at least ensure that it would not be abolished, because they feared that the Northern states would spread their industrial economy and exploit the South as a market for their goods. Cheap slave labor was the only thing keeping the South going. Several negotiations were formed throughout American history, like the 1820 Missouri Compromise, to ensure the continuance of slavery, but many Southern states considered negotiation impossible after the election of the abolitionist Presidential candidate Abraham Lincoln (1809-1865).

Lincoln had a brief political career before becoming President. He served one term in Congress in 1847, and then withdrew from politics until slavery became the dominant issue, running for Senate in 1858. Lincoln had a profound hatred of slavery and grief over its existence, and helped form the Republican Party to support the abolition of slavery. Lincoln rode the rising abolitionist sentiments and the more severe division between North and South to the Presidency in 1860. During the campaign, the Democratic Party had broken apart; the Northern Democrats refused to promote slavery. Southern states, beginning with South Carolina, began seceding within days of Lincoln's election. Seven states formed themselves into the Confederacy and made Jefferson Davis their President. Lincoln refused to acknowledge the validity of this response, and dedicated himself to keeping the Union together. When Lincoln affirmed this view by sending food to Fort Sumter, after South Carolina had demanded that it surrender the federal land to it, the Confederate troops fired on the fort, and on April 12, 1861, the Civil War began.

Four more states joined the Confederacy, with Virginia breaking in two, part for the South, and West Virginia for the North. The most famous Northern commanders were Ulysses S. Grant (1822-1885) and William Sherman (1820-1891). Grant led

Abraham Lincoln had undertaken the American Civil War primarily as a moral and political struggle, with the goal of ending slavery.

Illinois troops in the Western area at the beginning of the conflict, and won decisive battles at Vicksburg and Chattanooga, resulting in his promotion to General-in-chief. Grant appointed Sherman the head of the Western Union forces, and sent him to attack Georgia. Sherman is famous for his employment of "total war." Upon taking Atlanta, the state capitol, in 1864, he evacuated the city, and began his famous "March to the Sea" to capture the port of Savannah. During the march, his troops consumed or destroyed everything they came across, burning houses and tearing up railroads. After taking Savannah, Sherman continued to the Carolinas on the coast, and met up with Grant's army that was attacking Virginia. General Robert E. Lee (1807-1870), the most famous Southern commander and General-in-chief of the Confederacy, had fought and lost at the decisive Battle of Gettysburg in Pennsylvania. Despite his strategic brilliance, his diminishing army forced him to retreat from Richmond, VA, the Confederate capitol, before Grant's assault. It was Lee that finally surrendered to Grant in Appomattox, VA, on April 9, 1865.

In addition to the military victories, a decisive turning point in the war was the Emancipation Proclamation, which Lincoln issued on Sept 22, 1862. It consisted of an executive order that freed all slaves in Confederate States that refused to rejoin the Union, effective Jan 1st. Lincoln had undertaken the war primarily as a moral and political struggle. He wanted to end slavery, but sold the war to the North as an attempt to preserve the Union. The Proclamation made the end of slavery a major goal of the war. The order immediately freed all runaway slaves that were being held by the Union, and positively impacted the morale of Southern slaves. The Union Army was bolstered by the enlistment of thousands of newly freed slaves. Lincoln also pushed for a 13th Amendment to the Constitution that would abolish slavery everywhere, and it was eventually ratified in December 1865. Lincoln, however, did not see the end of slavery to which he had committed his career. Five days after winning the Civil War, Lincoln was shot in the back of the head by John Wilkes Booth while watching a show at the theater.

One of the popular stories about the Civil War is the operation of the "underground railroad," a series of secret routes, tunnels, and safe houses that allowed slaves to move from the South to the North, where they were considered free, or even as far as Canada. The Underground Railroad became largely ineffective after the Fugitive Slave Laws were made stricter in 1850, forcing local officials help slave hunters looking for runaways. But contemporary American schoolchildren are taught about the Underground Railroad as an example of the bravery of the African Americans and White Southerners in opposing the institution of slavery. The best TV series that shows the Civil War is North and South, although it is kind of a love story, but one will understand American history very well.

Chapter 8

"*They say that time changes things, but you actually have to change them yourself.*"

Andy Warhol, AMERICAN ARTIST, (1928-1987)

. . . .

DAY SEVENTY THREE :: MONDAY
NOVEMBER 24, 2008

"The vision is really about empowering workers, giving them all the information about what's going on so they can do a lot more than they've done in the past."

— Bill Gates, American entrepreneur, (1955-)

Whenever I get a chance I call my family, and today I called my brother Humood who was with my brother Ahmed at the time. Both of them are very interested in the American economy in general and specifically would also like to find an opportunity to expand their businesses. We talked about the American stock market, and we noticed that the ups and downs in Saudi stock market follow the ups and downs in the U.S. within 5-7 days. So I advised them to trade in the Saudi market based on what happened in the American stock market, taking into consideration the one week gap.

149

The whole world is becoming a small business market. What happens in one part of the world influences the rest of the world within a very short time. For example, when the oil price went up in 2007 to almost $150 a barrel, the worst impact was on Saudis. Because Saudis import so many goods, prices of everything rose; yet, Americans and others think that individual Saudis benefit from higher oil prices.

. . . .

DAY SEVENTY FOUR :: TUESDAY
NOVEMBER 25, 2008

"Religion is to do right. It is to love, it is to serve, it is to think, and it is to be humble."

— Ralph Waldo Emerson, American poet, (1803-1882)

Kristen picked me up at seven and we went to her friend's home. Her friend used to run a small restaurant specialized in vegan food but she closed it down and ended up having her selected friends and customers coming over to have dinner at her home. She cooked for about 15-20 people every Tuesday and charged $30 per person. It was a special Tuesday when Kristen invited me because it was two days before Thanksgiving and so she served a vegan Thanksgiving dinner. Two of Kristen's close friends joined us at the table and we talked for an hour about veganism. Later on, another close friend of Kristen, who is a real estate agent, joined us for dessert and tea. We switched the topic to the current real estate situation, a disastrous situation in America. I remember when I bought a home in VA in 1998, I paid about one-hundred-sixty-thousand, and I sold it four years later for two-hundred-fifty thousand. The real estate in America rises about five to seven percent yearly, and every seven years there is a loop when the real estate jumps about twenty percent. Luckily, I bought that home a year before the loop, and that's why its price almost doubled. When I checked its price these days, I found it appraised at about three-hundred-thousand but, according to standard increase, it should exceed four-hundred-thousand.

. . ..

DAY SEVENTY FIVE :: WEDNESDAY
NOVEMBER 26, 2008

"They say that time changes things, but you actually have to change them yourself."
— Andy Warhol, American artist, (1928-1987)

At Friday prayer, I met a member of al-Furqan Foundation. This foundation focuses on publishing the Holy Quran although they do sell some other Islamic books. What grabbed my attention was the way workers for this organization live what I would call "American Islam." The employers there are from the second or third generation of Muslim Indo/Pakistani background families. They seem to have no problem whatsoever living comfortably with American culture. They manage to perform their religious rituals without experiencing difficult contradictions. They also maintain some of their own cultural tradition. For example, in their neighborhood there are Indo/Pakistani stores and restaurants. They attend good colleges and do well. At the same time they manage to attend weekend school where they learn their language and gain religious instruction. This balancing is different, and much better than those who try to be disconnected with either their background or American culture.

Some new immigrant Muslims and Arabs will encourage their children to speak English and have them make friends beyond their ethnic group, adopting the American style of food, music, and clothing. On the other hand, there are those who try to keep separate from the larger American society to the extent that they run their own schools, restaurants, social activities, etc. In America, most immigrants or visitors from Muslim countries are educated or they are there to obtain college degree. So, they are confident about their belief and culture, but still want to make sure to retain their Muslim identity.

. . ..

DAY SEVENTY SIX :: THURSDAY
NOVEMBER 27, 2008
"Music should be something that makes you gotta move, inside or outside."
— Elvis Presley, American singer, (1935-1977)

America is quiet today. Few people are outside or working. For me it seems like a sad quietness. Inside the houses, however, people gather with joy. My cousin Bader Almugayel from Ohio and I accepted Professor Aana's invitation for Thanksgiving dinner. Her apartment was full of people; her family, her friends, her neighbors. The apartment was also packed with plenty of different homemade food as everyone contributed to the large meal, adding to the huge Turkey Aana prepared. Most importantly, her home was full of joy, happiness, and love. Her teenage nieces and nephews were very sociable, raising smart questions, and demonstrating in-depth knowledge of geography that surprised me. More interesting were their questions about Saudi Arabia. They asked about teenagers' activities in Saudi Arabia. They were surprised when they learned that my eight-year-old daughter, Nouf, enjoyed learning how to bake cakes and helped take care of her young infant brother, Abdulrahman, in addition to playing with such electronic games as Game Boy, Play Station (PS3), Wii, etc. She also enjoys attending parties and gatherings with other girls her age. The boys also have these electronic games, but they would play soccer and do outdoor activities instead of having parties. For example, my older son, Abdulaziz, would spend hours playing PS3 if I let him, while my second son, Muhammad, is always busy with outdoor activities. Next they asked about Bader and me and other people our age. I explained that we also enjoyed some sports activities. For example, Bader organizes volleyball teams and we enjoy playing at his place twice a week in addition to other social activities we have.

The evening was spent visiting different clubs with a student from the Theology Department who offered to show me around and take me with some of her friends to different styles of dance clubs, such as Goth, Hip-hop, and Punk. Hip-hop, or Rap, was invented in the 1970s by Clive Campbell, called DJ Kool Herc. While playing records at dance parties, Herc set up two turntables so he could play the most rhythmic sections of a song over and over, and would shout over the music to the dancers. These two elements formed the basis of every Hip-hop song to come. A Hip-hop song is composed of a "beat," the background music and a drum beat, and the lyrics. They can be very simple or incredibly complex: one album produced by Prince Paul sampled seventy-six songs for twenty-one tracks. Today, Hip-hop production uses a few samples per song, or uses synthesizers or a live band to produce samples.

Hip-hop lyrics have consistently been the object of controversy. Most rappers are

151

▲ *Chicago*

(Left) Cousins Bader Almugayel and Fahad Alhomoudi are represented in the Chicago Bean in Millennium Park.

(Right) Bader, Fahad, Benjamin, Aana, and her mother Alison stand in front of the Chicago Bean in Millennium Park.

African American and come from an inner-city environment surrounded by crime and poverty. When they began to write songs about their lives and homes, these songs were interpreted as glorifying a criminal lifestyle. Rap group N.W.A., for example, was denounced for recording songs about shooting the police and buying cocaine. In reality, however, these songs were criticizing police brutality and the exploitation of Black men through addiction.

While some rap does celebrate breaking the law, abusing women, and getting money, socially-conscious Rap has been instrumental in bringing attention to the contemporary struggles of African Americans and bringing Black artists to national prominence. Rappers like KRS-One angrily condemn the degenerate living conditions and institutional abuse of Black men and women. They also form positive images of Black America, and inspire their fans to overcome the destructive lifestyle that racism and marginalization produce in African Americans.

Beside Rap, there is Rock 'n' Roll, a style of popular music that originated in America. Influenced by Jazz, Blues, Gospel and Country, Rock 'n' Roll is usually played with a guitar, bass, keyboard and drums. But, it can employ anything from harmonicas to flutes or entire symphonies. Most Rock songs last three or four minutes, but some "progressive rock" bands have recorded songs as long as forty-five minutes. Rock 'n' Roll has numerous variations: Beach, Punk, Metal, Prog, Hair, Jock, Indie, Alternative, Soft, etc. But all of these types employ a strong backbeat and brisk tempo to keep the listener's interest.

One of the earliest Rock 'n' Roll artists was Elvis Presley (1935-1977), named the "King of Rock 'n' Roll." His music mixed traditional southern styles with fast tempos complemented by his powerful, distinctive voice. It also incorporated many elements of African American music, thereby introducing Black music to a mainstream White audience. Presley's African American influences, plus his erotic on-stage movements, provoked controversy and made Presley a symbol of youth culture. It also contributed to Rock 'n' Roll's character as the music of rebellion against mainstream culture.

Presley's offenses quickly paled in the light of the '60s. Rock 'n' Roll allied itself with movements encouraging sexual liberality, criticizing religion, and advocating the use of illegal drugs. The music of the Beatles, a British band that came to America in 1964, helped form a counter-culture that opposed the government, protested Christianity, and the Vietnam War, while embracing a loosely Eastern spiritual vision of love and personal freedom. Long after the Beatles have dissolved, Rock 'n' Roll still defines itself as a rejection of the dominant tradition and an affirmation of the values of American youth.

These Pop American and Western Pop culture influenced the entire world, but it did not reach the third world countries until years later. I vividly remember when I was a kid in the early '80s that my mom used to warn me against having long hair because those who have long hair imitate the Beatles and they are careless about morality and tradition, and at that time I had no clue about the Beatles. Until now, the West, and America in particular, has great influence on my country and many other countries all over the world. With the modern technology American cultural trends reach us much faster. What exists in America will be practiced among Saudi youth within weeks. It is not only the economic situation but also the pop culture that Saudis will imitate.

153

I am nearing the end of this ICAP Fulbright Program and have one more trip to make, this time to San Francisco to visit Berkeley.

. . . .

DAY SEVENTY SEVEN :: FRIDAY
November 28, 2008
"Imagination is more important than knowledge. For knowledge is limited to all we now know and understand, while imagination embraces the entire world, and all there ever will be to know and understand."
— Albert Einstein, American physicist, (1879-1955)

Since its opening in July 2004, Millennium Park has hosted millions of people, making it one of the most popular destinations in Chicago. The Cloud Gate or "the bean" as it is nicknamed by locals is the most fascinating piece of art in the Park. This piece, built in 2004 and completed May 15, 2006, has no fixed identity, but rather occupies an illusionary space that is consistent with eastern theologies shared by Buddhism, Hinduism, and Taoism, as well as Albert Einstein's views of a non-three-dimensional world. Anish Kapoor, the Indian artist who designed the Cloud Gate, explored the theme of ambiguity with his work that places the viewer in a state of "in-betweenness."

By looking at this piece of art I realized how great America is. It took a tremendous amount of time and effort to create this artwork. The Cloud Gate represents the American Culture. It is designed by a British-born Indian artist. In 1999, Millennium Park officials and a group of art collectors and architects reviewed the artistic works of thirty different artists, and selected Kapoor's design. This selection demonstrates how to select projects and individuals based on the quality of their work above other considerations. The cost for the piece was first estimated at $6 million but the final figure was $23 million in 2006. No public funds were involved; all funding came from donations from individuals and corporations. This positive partnership between the private business companies and the public is again exemplary. Chicagoans and many tourists enjoy spending weekends at the Millennium Park. While there, I suddenly heard my name being called. Bader and I wondered who could possibly recognize us. We were so surprised to turn and meet Professor Aana with her family near the Cloud Gate. We all enjoyed the coincidence, took pictures together and thanked each other for the wonderful Thanksgiving dinner we had shared.

After Asif Khan completed a nice tour for us, he invited my cousin Bader Almugayel and me to a dinner at his home where we met his family. Asif, like other Muslims and all immigrants I guess, is concerned about raising his children in the same manner he would raise them back home. He is even thinking seriously about moving to a Muslim country for a decade or so until his children go through the teenage phase of their life. At Asif's house you would know that you are at a house of an American of Indian decent. While the house design and furniture is similar to all American houses, the decoration, pictures and pieces of art are from India. Even the music they play, the scent of their home and the food are Indian. I found the homemade Indian food much better than what I had eaten at Indian restaurants. Although Asif works in the financial sector, his love of art and paintings occupies much of his time. Like many Americans do when they have a particular interest, Asif has developed his own website to share his interest with others

Later on, I met Bader at my office at Loyola and we took a walk down by the lake. We reflected on the situation of Saudis who had interacted with Americans compared to those who have never allowed themselves to be exposed to people of other faiths and cultures. We agreed that there is great benefit in engaging in open dialogue and exchange of ideas about life and religion noting that for immigrant Muslims, the distinction between religion and culture was crucial. It would be possible to assimilate to American culture while reserving religious practices, but immigrant Muslims who would cling tightly to traditional culture would likely find great dif ficulty living in America. He felt strongly that it was much better for them to engage and adapt to American culture and practices as long as it wouldn't contradict their beliefs.

In addition to being exposed to others, Bader acknowledges that the changes King

Abdullah has made through his interfaith and education initiatives have opened the eyes of Saudis. In fact these changes are causing a rapid paradigm shift by providing profound motivation for getting to know and appreciate other cultures.

Bader remembered that while he was a student during the 1990s most of his peers would have found it difficult to engage in dialogue with people of other faiths. But, after visiting some religious places like the Quaker church, he appreciates the similarities and therefore recommended that Saudi students get to know Americans at school and beyond, on a personal level. He felt strongly that treating one another with respect and recognition would lead to a mutual respect of culture and beliefs, a necessary component of peaceful coexistence.

. .. .

DAY EIGHTY :: MONDAY
DECEMBER 1, 2008
"The liberties of our country, the freedom of our civil constitution, are worth defending against all hazards."

— Samuel Adams, American patriot, (1722-1803)

I arrived in Berkeley and traveled to meet the President and the Dean of Graduate Theological Union (GTU). The GTU is a world renowned, ecumenical consortium of nine schools, including Greek Orthodox to Judaic, Catholic, Islamic, and Buddhist Studies. The GTU brings together religious scholars from all over the world. The variety of these faith traditions provides a perfect climate for social and intellectual interchange on all levels. Students from any of these colleges can take courses in any affiliated institute within GTU, which makes it a significant place for interfaith dialogue. It is known for its high level of academic excellence and for being the largest partnership of seminaries and graduate schools in America.

GTU Member Schools are American Baptist Seminary of the West (ABSW), American Baptist Church, Church Divinity School of the Pacific (CDSP), Episcopal Church, Dominican School of Philosophy & Theology (DSPT), Roman Catholic Church, Franciscan School of Theology (FST), Roman Catholic Church, Jesuit School of Theology (JST), Roman Catholic Church, Pacific Lutheran Theological Seminary (PLTS), Evangelical Lutheran Church in America, Pacific School of Religion (PSR), Multi-denominational, San Francisco Theological Seminary (SFTS), Presbyterian Church (USA), and Starr King School for the Ministry (SKSM), and Unitarian Universalist. In addition to those members there are eleven academic centers, programs, and affiliates that allow the GTU to be a pioneering place for interdisciplinary religious thought, study, and practice, adding to its unparalleled depth of faculty and course selection.

. . ..

DAY EIGHTY ONE :: TUESDAY
DECEMBER 2, 2008
"Wealth is the ability to fully experience life."
— Henry David Thoreau, American philosopher and poet, (1817-1862)

I had to wake up early this morning and get ready to see as many of the colleges and professors at the GTU as I can. My first visit was to the Dominican Center where I learned about their legacy and tradition. Since its founding in 1216 by St. Dominic de Guzman, study has been held central to the life and work of the Dominican Order. Their tradition asserts that it is not possible to study theology without philosophy. In their methodology, philosophy not only forms a vital preparation for theology, but they take each subject seriously, for its own sake. This means that each discipline is always open to be influenced by the other. Like St. Thomas Aquinas, they are called to be open to the truth wherever it is found. He sought to understand the truth in all its forms and taught the critical relationship between faith and reason. In both philosophical and theological inquiry they emphasized not only understanding, but applying the truth in practice. Seeking the truth in this Dominican way helps me understand why they have a serious interest in studying Islam and even have a Muslim graduate student.

The Dominican School of Philosophy and Theology (DSPT) began when Francis Vilarrasa, O.P. brought six novices on a long journey to establish the Dominican Order on the West Coast of the United States in 1851. To prepare them for the priesthood, he opened a school in Monterey, which he later relocated to Benicia. Some eighty years later, the Master of the Order requested that they follow the Dominican tradition of being located near a major university. In 1932 the friars moved to Oakland, establishing the College of St. Albert the Great near the University of California at Berkeley.

Next I met with Franciscans. I had met a Franciscan fellow in Chicago whose dress caught my attention. He was wearing a long brown gown like the *thobe* we wear in Saudi Arabia, with a few robes over his shoulders. Since meeting this young man, I have wanted to know more about their beliefs and teaching. At their center I received a warm welcome, but only one professor was there, so I did not see anyone wearing Franciscan dress. I did see some who wore the robes in pictures on their publications. I also learned from their publications that this school goes all the way back to 1854 when Mission Santa Barbara was chartered as an apostolic college and continued in that capacity until 1885.

The mission of the school is to prepare candidates for professional ministry in the Roman Catholic Church. From 1869 to 1877, it also functioned as a college for laymen. In 1896, it began a four-year high school seminary program. The high school became a separate institution in 1901, and the college department became a separate institution at San Luis Rey, California, in 1929. Over the course of the years, the college department expanded into a four-year accredited liberal arts college. Mission Santa Barbara remained the center for theological studies and continued to operate as a seminary until 1968 when the theological school moved to Berkeley, California as the Franciscan School of Theology, a member school of the Graduate Theological Union. Now they are the only Franciscan seminary/theology school whose mission is to prepare professional ministers for the church. Guided and governed in its educational mission, the Franciscan School continues to bring the questions of contemporary culture, society, and church into dialogue with the ever-ancient and ever-new word of the gospel.

We went back to the Islamic Studies Department, and although they have been there for less than two years, they have developed a strong program due to two reasons. One is the young leader there who wants this department to be well-connected with its peers. Second, being located at GTU facilitates most of the administrative work. This strategy for a new school to piggy back existing schools happens often in the American system, offering students great advantages.

Later in the afternoon, the Director of the Islamic Studies Department took me to visit Telegraph Street. Telegraph Street is known for its human rights movements and activities. Everyone in Berkeley knows this street and I thought it would be known throughout the United States like they know Las Vegas for example. To my surprise I found out this was not the case. Someone explained to me that major streets in a city would only be known to local people unless someone had traveled to many cities. As I thought about it, I realized how much sense this fact made for a country like America with 50 states and 350 million people.

Late in the evening I headed back to Chicago very aware of the wealth of new friendships as greater than financial wealth.

. .. .

DAY EIGHTY TWO :: WEDNESDAY
DECEMBER 3, 2008
"The most I can do for my friend is simply be his friend."
　　　　　— Henry David Thoreau, American philosopher and poet, (1817-1862)

W hat I like most about the places I have visited and the people I have met are the friendships I have made over this short period of time, especially with intellectuals and families. Today, I received what I consider to be the fruit of my trip. When I opened my email box, I found a letter from Professor Dennis Martin with important information.

Fahad,

Here are five internet sites that I would recommend as giving the conservative side of things. They vary widely and I would not endorse everything that appears on them; some of what appears on them I would disagree with. But they do give one an opportunity to get analysis of news that one won't find in The New York Times or Washington Post.

http://www.wsj.com/   *http://www.washingtontimes.com/*
http://www.americanthinker.com/   *http://www.nationalreview.com/*
http://townhall.com/

I am attaching an article that ran in one the newspapers. It goes back to the first lunch you had with several of us faculty members. I have seen a number of similar reports about how Christians in Saudi Arabia are subject to harassment and may not be entirely free to practice their faith privately. A number of these reports referred especially to Filipino or other Christian workers living in Saudi Arabia temporarily, reports of some of them being arrested and treated very badly simply for privately practicing their faith. I know that these accounts may be inaccurate and I do understand that the pressure against even private practice of non-Muslim religion is coming from extremist elements within the country. In other words, even from the attached article I can see that the government makes some effort to protect private practice of the Christian faith in Saudi Arabia. However, some of the accounts I have read do leave me very concerned because they seem to say that the principle that people are free to practice other religions privately is not always upheld. Perhaps this article at least gives you an idea of what concerns some Americans who pay attention to news from the Middle East and why they are a bit suspicious of the defense that freedom for private practice of religion exists but that the government could not protect Christians if they were permitted to practice their religion publicly. It seems to some people here as if the underlying problem is the growth and flourishing of extremist forms of Islam within Saudi Arabia; they wonder why that is permitted. In the end, it all comes back to the question of true religious freedom, whether one has real freedom of religion if public practice is not permitted, and whether the prohibition of public practice doesn't actually encourage animosity toward the proscribed faiths.

But having said all that, I also must say that when you gave the answer you did (that it's a security issue), it helped me to see this article in a different light. I can see that the priest who is interviewed here said much the same thing you said. I would perhaps have missed some aspects of what he said had I not heard your answer. So thank you.

All of these are big questions that are hard to answer and you are not responsible for the policies that exist today any more than I am responsible for the policies of the U.S. government today. I have nothing but respect for your sincere interfaith openness and applaud you for your efforts. May your work in interfaith conversation flourish. It was a privilege to meet you and talk with you.

Once more, thank you for your interest in things American. Your desire to find out and understand things is admirable. May God bless you as you return to your homeland.

Dennis Martin

158

The issue we were discussing was about the freedom of religion in Islam in general and in Saudi Arabia in particular. There is no compulsion in religion as stated clearly in the Quran. In Saudi Arabia, the majority of the population is Sunni Muslims, and as far as I know Shi'i Muslims do practice their rituals. They have their own mosques in the Eastern region and have their own imams. They are not allowed, however, to practice public rituals that contradict with the Islamic law, the applied law in Saudi Arabia. The same is true for the Sufi Muslims.

In the evening I had a farewell dinner with William French, the head of the department, and a few others. One of the professors came late because she had a Music class. She has been studying music since she was six-years-old, and she is almost sixty-years-old now. Music plays a big role in American and Christian culture, generally speaking, as it is part of their religious practices. That's why we find music departments in the religion schools of many American universities. I think that music in Christianity can replace the textual reading. In Judaism, they still read the Torah and observe its rituality; it is the holy script of God. In Islam, both the Torah and musical instruments and rituals were replaced by the Quran, an orally transmitted text.

In my humble opinion, there are three different forms of order or revelation; in Judaism the written texts, i.e., Torah, with its rabbinical interpretation, and Muslims believe that God sent the scroll to Moses. In Christianity, Jesus was the word of God; even Muslims believe that Jesus was the word which has the spirit of God. Therefore, for Christians, following Jesus is the way to God. The prayers in Christianity were formed and presented through musical instruments, beginning with Gregorian III who wrote a specific note for each prayer, and then the musical notes and prayers developed in Christianity. In Islam, Quran comes as the final word of God. Prophet Muhammad, peace be upon him, prevented his followers from reading the Judaic texts, and from listening to music which represents religious practices in Christianity. However, many Muslims do not distinguish between songs and music, and they think both are equally forbidden.

Chapter 9

"*I've learned that people will forget what you said, people will forget what you did, but people will never forget how you made them feel.*"

Maya Angelou, AMERICAN POET, (1928-)

. . ..

DAY EIGHTY THREE :: THURSDAY
DECEMBER 4, 2008

"Members of the U.S. House and the U.S. Senate are not there by accident. Each managed to get there for some reason. Learn what it was and you will know something important about them, about our country and about the American people."

—Donald Rumsfeld, American Secretary of Defense, (1932-)

This morning I headed to Washington D.C. I spent the first day sightseeing, including visits to the White House, Congress, House of Representatives, and the Jefferson, Lincoln, and Roosevelt Memorials. I wondered about the selection of those three Presidents, and I wanted to learn more, choosing Roosevelt as a model.

161

Franklin Delano Roosevelt (1882-1945) got an early boost in politics from being the nephew of President Theodore Roosevelt; in 1910, he was the first Democratic elected to state senate for his heavily Republican district in 26 years. In 1921 he lost the use of his legs to polio, but still managed to not appear in public in his wheelchair during the race for Governor of New York in 1928; indeed, after teaching himself to walk using iron braces and a cane, he never appeared openly in a wheelchair until 1945. He roundly defeated Herbert Hoover, whose attempts to end the Depression had largely failed, in the 1932 Presidential election, and held the office for an unmatched four terms (a feat declared illegal soon after he died). Roosevelt was a dynamic and energetic personality who represented to the American people the vigor with which they rose to the challenge of the Depression. Especially popular were his "Fireside Chats," which were radio addresses made in a friendly and popular manner that encouraged Americans to support the New Deal programs.

The Roosevelt administration faced two serious challenges: the Depression and the rise of Hitler. In response to the Depression, Roosevelt worked with Congress to pass massive and sweeping legislation as soon as he was inaugurated, a period of activity that is the origin for the "first hundred days" criteria used to measure later Presidents. The government passed laws to regulate industrial competition, shut down and reorganize banks, establish a federal agency to ensure bank deposits, subsidize farms, establish Social Security, and fund public works to manage unemployment. This legislative agenda is referred to as the New Deal. Despite the fact that he led the first major government intervention into the American economy, Roosevelt was actually reluctant to agree to such vast expenditure, and remained concerned with balancing the budget.

Roosevelt was concerned about Hitler early on, and began to turn American opinion away from isolationism. Roosevelt was so dedicated to aiding Britain and France against German forces that, when faced with a weapons embargo that forbid flying planes from

American airfields to combatant countries, he planned to divert the planes to Canada and sell them to France. Roosevelt got as far as the 1941 Lend-Lease Act, which allowed the President to sell or lease weapons at their discretion, when Pearl Harbor decisively involved America in World War II. Roosevelt created numerous war committees and bureaucracies, involving himself directly with the war strategy, although not always very effectively. Before his death, Roosevelt participated in the 1945 Yalta conference with Britain and Russia to plan out post-war Germany and begin developing the United Nations, effectively ending the era of American Isolationism.

After sightseeing we had dinner at an Argentinean restaurant. I went to write in my journal at a café at Dupont Circle. This circle, I realize, is famous for being a gay circle. In most North American cities, gays have their own part of the city. It is more obvious in some cities like Montreal, where gays have their own gay village with all kinds of shops, restaurants and cafes. The gay shops are identified by the seven colors of the rainbow.

. .. .

DAY EIGHTY FOUR: FRIDAY
DECEMBER 5, 2008
"We cannot set up, out of our heads, something we regard as the ideal society. We must base our conception upon societies which actually exist, in order to have any assurance that our ideal is a practicable one."

— John Dewey, American philosopher, (1859-1952)

The last conference in ICAP was at the Catholic University of America. The Dean of Theology and Religious Studies opened the first session after lunch. He was proud of Pope Benedict's visit last year. The debriefing was attended by Bureau of Educational and Cultural Affairs, among them the Managing Director of Academic Programs and Chief of European and Eurasian Program Branch, Benedict Duffy.

Dr. Leonard Swidler presented the opening lecture, addressing the need for dialogue among the Abrahamic religions, namely Judaism, Christianity, and Islam. The dialogue evolved around four words starting with C; Creed, Code of behavior, Cult, and Community structure. The three religions have qualities that differentiate them from all other beliefs, in that they turn people toward this world, while other religions and beliefs try to keep people away from this life. Swidler thinks that Salvation grabs people's attention toward this world while all other religions: Hinduism, Buddhism, Judaism, etc., do not.

The embrace of dialogue brings us to another topic here, as dialogue brings humans to their higher life, which Swidler calls the cosmic dance of dialogue. Nowadays we cannot ignore the others because we live in one small world. In the past we tried to force others to live our lives. But now, there are three types of dialogue; dialogue of the head, dialogue of the heart, and dialogue of the hands. While the dialogue of the head is built on understanding, the most effective dialogue is found in the dialogue of the heart, then the dialogue of the hands which is derived from the heart, and guides us to the holy and to the wholeness of humans.

As Swidler was talking about the cosmic dance, more students came in and sat on my table in the back. I usually sit on the nearest table to an outlet so that I can plug in my computer and type the summary of the lecture. Swidler launched the *Journal of Ecumenical Studies* in early '60s. Then in 1974, he established the center for dialogue at Temple University. At that time there were 12 Muslim scholars were willing to participate in dialogue; now hundreds of Muslim scholars are participating in different kinds of dialogue and, as he said, we have six of them at this lecture. The word *dialogue* comes from the Greek root "dia" and "logue," "dia" means cross and "logue" means meaning or word, so dialogue means crossing the words or meanings. Swidler repeated that we should begin the dialogue by building trust, knowing that all religions claim Abraham and monotheism.

After the lecture, Julie led dialogue with the Fulbrighters based on the lecture. Julie and Rebecca asked the Fulbrighters about the special moment they would like to share with others, so with the dialogue of the head, Muhammad and Ghassan shared their experience during the election. Then, with the dialogue of the heart Serge shared how he felt about his experience of his first communion service led by a woman. Mousse had a similar comment that he shared with us and it was more of a hope than an experience that he would see more Muslim women participating in congregations. The story I shared about the dialogue of the hand was about my visit with Aana Vigen. As Thanksgiving was getting closer, I thought I would be stuck in my apartment because everything would be closed and everyone would be busy with their families so I called my cousin who was in Ohio and asked him to come to Chicago so we could enjoy our time during this break. But then, a few days before Thanksgiving, Aana invited me to join their families for dinner. It was not all about the delicious turkey we had, but about people gathering from all religions to thank God for what He has provided for us. After a few questions about these stories, we had a coffee break.

The first breakout session had two panels; Panel I about NGOs and Interfaith Dialogue, and Panel II about Diversity and Interfaith Initiatives. The second panel attracted me more, so I attended the panel and the first speaker was Ziad who focused on diversity in Lebanon. Then Justin Baird gave a presentation about Jewish dialogue in America and American dialogue. Sara Curran discussed her own experience, then Fatima Hussein shared her personal experience as well, including many lectures and social activities, but what she liked most is her encounter with the Shi'i mosque which was her first direct contact with Shi'i because Indonesia was a Sunni dominant country. The lecturer who represented the last panel comes from a very diverse family, i.e., from a Jewish father and Quaker mother. Mousse was sitting next to me and whenever the

163

lecturer referred to Fatima by Dr. Hussein he would look at me and laugh repeating what the lecturer just said "Dr. Hussein." We always referred to her as Fatima, and generally speaking Arabs go by the first name, so he found the reference awkward.

. . ..

DAY EIGHTY FIVE :: SATURDAY
DECEMBER 6, 2008
"I've learned that people will forget what you said, people will forget what you did, but people will never forget how you made them feel."

— Maya Angelou, American poet, (1928-)

Tink Tinker delivered today's plenary lecture. Tinker explained his differing view of dialogue by describing what it is like *eing haoka*. It means that one goes through one's day being oriented to activities from the right side. For example, when Tink puts on his shoes, he puts on the right one first and when he goes to bed at night, he sleeps on the right side facing the East. *Maoka*, another Native American tribe, is oriented in daily life toward the left side. These differences are what make balance in the world more than dialogue. Because the word sacred does not exist in Native American language, these assumptions and practices are not considered sacred.

Tinker also spoke about religious violence, saying that religion is the source of violence in the world. When Columbus came to the Americas, he found over forty-million Native Americans already living in the land. A census of thirty years ago showed that number to be down to less than a million. Native American populations are back up to three and a half million now. By contrast, Native Americans have never committed such genocide. Tinker finds American foreign policy so violent; therefore, he is interested in learning about other religions' views on violence, including Islam.

His interest would have found informative responses in the first panel of the day entitled "Toward a Global Ethic: Interfaith Dialogue Beyond Cultural Borders." My presentation at the panel was about ethics from an Islamic perspective. I included three stories in my presentation; the first two were about the Prophet and one was a personal story, as I have learned Americans tend to like stories. The first story related to the prophet was that "the Prophet, peace be upon him, went from Medina to Mecca, and when he reached a place in between them called Athayah, he saw a wounded deer standing in a shadow of a sand hill, with an arrow in his body. The Prophet told one of his companions to stand next to the deer so as the deer wouldn't be frightened, until the prophet and the caravan had passed by." The second prophetic story was about his companion ibn Masoud. When ibn Masoud and some other companions were traveling with the Prophet, peace be upon him, the Prophet went away, and ibn Masoud saw a red bird with its two young ones so he took them away from their mother. Then the bird came fluttering down to the ground. When the Prophet returned, he asked the companion: "Who distressed this bird by taking away its young ones? Return them to where they came from." I asked the audience if they had ever heard these two stories before. As I expected, no one had heard them. In fact, even when I teach Muslim students at the school of law, I find them unaware of this kind of prophetic tradition regarding the environment and animal rights. Plenty of materials exist that relate to environment, animal rights and other global common values, but they are not widely circulated.

The three other panelists spoke on similar themes. William French seconded me on the importance of choosing neutral topics that are of common interest to discuss in dialogue among differing religious and political interests. The last panelist to present was Mehre Niknam. Mehri narrated a few stories from the Jewish tradition, one of which is that when one takes eggs from the nest then one should not take them when the mother bird is there and also one should not take all the eggs. One must leave at least one egg for the mother otherwise the mother will suffer and the balance and sustainability of the environment will be negatively affected. She concluded her stories with a story of Rabbi Hillel who lived just before the time of Jesus. Hillel once told his students that they should care about themselves and others, stating "if I do not take care of myself, who will? And if I care only about myself, then who am I? And if I do not do that now, then when?" Both her stories corroborated mine in a common assumption about dialogue helping to forward genuine collaboration on serious global concerns. Our presentations were made stronger in both our minds by the differences we represented: She had come from the U.K. and was of Iranian descent and I was from Saudi Arabia; she had been educated in Shi'i society and I in a Wahhabi one; she is Jewish and I am Muslim; she is a woman and I a man.

The last lecture of the day confirmed this plea to engage common human values. Muddaser spoke to the Muslim understanding that God could have created the whole of humanity as one religion, with one culture and no differences. Instead, God created the various nations and tribes to encourage recognition of each other. Muslims are required to pursue mutual and harmonious co-existence with followers of other religions and to forge ties with them on the basis of their belief in one God and common human values.

On this last day in the States, I made an effort to go shopping for my family back home. I tried to decide which mall to go to, Pentagon Mall or Tyson's Corner Mall, but I went to the first one because it was closer. The mall had not changed much since my last visit years ago. I called my wife, Sarah, to consult with her on gifts and to reminisce about our home when we lived in Virginia. I also described for her the beautiful huge Christmas tree in the middle of the mall and the other preparations for Christmas, even though we were still in early December. Americans now start the preparation for Christmas as early as early November.

Christmas, held every year on December 25, is the most important holiday in

American culture. It originates in a traditional Christian celebration of the birth of Jesus, but has expanded into both a federally recognized holiday and major social event. It also roughly coincides with the Jewish celebration of Hanukah and the African American celebration of Kwanzaa, December 26-January 1, which honors African heritage. As a result, most institutions will schedule winter breaks or generic "holiday parties" during the Christmas season. But both religious and nonreligious Americans appreciate Christmas as a time to remember and encourage goodwill.

Christmas has developed its own mythology apart from the religious significance. The most important figure is Santa Claus, a fat, white-bearded man dressed in a red coat, who rides a sleigh over the world to deliver presents to good children. Parents will tell children that the gifts they receive are from him, and many shopping centers will have actors dress like Santa so that children can tell him what they want. Further, there are numerous songs and television shows that portray other popular figures like Rudolph the Red-Nosed Reindeer and Frosty the Snowman. New immigrant Muslims find difficulties during Christmas time, because their kids will start to talk and sing and wait for Santa Claus to bring them gifts, and the parents worry about the influence of American culture on their culture and religion. Many of these same people will, however, acculturate and in a few years after their arrival will adopt Christmas as a cultural event and buy gifts for their children. Even though I don't believe in Christmas, I find it the best time to shop, as I love to shop.

Christmas is celebrated with parties, parades, and vacations from work. Many people visit their families during this time and give gifts to loved ones. Christian churches will hold special night services, concerts of Christmas music, or put on children's pageants. Americans also like to decorate their houses by putting strings of lights around the doors and roofs, or putting up decorations like wreaths, boughs of holly, and large inflatable Santas.

Many Americans think Christmas has become over-commercialized. People say that buying presents, throwing parties, and decorations have overshadowed the spirit of kindness or religious meaning of the holidays. But despite their objections, Christmas remains one of the most important events for businesses during the year.

Winter breaks for Christmas generally extend through New Year's Day which happens six days later. Many Americans hold New Year's Eve parties, watching various television specials featuring music and memories of the previous year playing in the background.

*Christmas has developed its own mythology apart from the religious significance,
including figures such as Santa Claus (left) and decorations such as lighted
evergreen trees (right), like this one in front of the U.S. Capitol Building.*

New York has the most famous New Year's celebration, held in Times Square, where
partiers cheer while a large metal sphere covered in light bulbs is lowered along a pole,
reaching the ground at the precise moment of the New Year.

After I finished shopping, I called one of my old friends whose wife taught me two
statistic courses at NOVA, Northern Virginia Community College. She picked up the
phone and recognized my voice, although I took her course over eight years ago. She
reminded me of a quiz she gave to her students and nobody got it right except me and
the answer was based on the fact that zero has a value. Now I know what a wonderful
feeling it is that students have when their teachers remember them. I will try not to forget
any of my students, but I know I am not very successful in fulfilling this intention.

167

. . . .

DAY EIGHTY SIX :: SUNDAY
DECEMBER 7, 2008

*"If ye love wealth greater than liberty, the tranquility of servitude greater than the animating
contest for freedom, go home from us in peace. We seek not your counsel, nor your arms.
Crouch down and lick the hand that feeds you. May your chains set lightly upon you; and
may posterity forget that ye were our countrymen."*
— Samuel Adams, American patriot, (1722-1803)

For my last breakfast with the ICAP group, I had American pancakes served
with maple syrup and honey. This breakfast reminded me of my breakfasts
with my parents because my dad loves honey with his breakfast. So I asked
the concierge where to find the best honey and he directed me to the farmer's
market at Dupont Circle. American farmers sell their products on Sunday markets in
different public places in each town. Before I went to the market, I went to Serge in
his room to say goodbye because he had not joined us for breakfast. Then I headed
to the airport with some Arab students whom I knew when I was in Virginia, and
while waiting for my plane, I had a lengthy conversation with my friends about
Muslim Arab Americans after 9-11. To my surprise, most of these Arabs didn't
go to mosques. More often the Indians and Muslims of other nations keep going
to pray and do activities collectively. I also heard stories about Saudi students who
were asked to leave the USA before completing their degrees. These stories detract
new Saudi students from obtaining their degrees from the USA. Still, over twenty-
thousand Saudi students are pursuing their undergraduate and graduate degrees
in different states. I worry though, that most of these young Saudi students love
and enjoy the life they are living in the USA without an in-depth understanding
of the American Culture. They get a taste of it without absorbing the history and
background behind the scenes.

. .. .

DAY EIGHTY SEVEN: MONDAY
DECEMBER 8, 2008

"America is always on the move. She may be going to Hell, of course, but at least she isn't standing still."

— E. E. Cummings quotes, American poet (1894-1962)

I have returned home to Saudi Arabia. Everyone was anxious to know about America more than they wanted to know about the details of my trip. Many questions were asked of me about the way Americans treat people at the airport, in stores, and streets, etc. They also wanted to know about the economy crisis; the situation of Saudis, Arabs and Muslims; the terrorists' effect on public life; the real estate market; and the price of merchandise. From their questions I can now better understand just how much the media and stereotyped stories have influenced their ideas and positions towards America and all things American. Whatever I tried to say to give a more accurate picture often fell on deaf ears, even when I spoke about the Americans electing Obama. Hopefully, King Abdullah's scholarship program, funding more than one-hundred-thousand Saudi students will help over time.

. .. .

DAY EIGHTY EIGHT :: TUESDAY
DECEMBER 9, 2008

"Sometimes questions are more important than answers."

— Nancy Willard, American poet, (1936-)

My trip has born many fruits, in addition to the continuous intellectual discussion I now have with some professors I met. I am writing this book first in English and then in Arabic to help allay misunderstandings. I am helping to organize several international conferences related to Interfaith Dialogue, Islamic Law, and Environment. I am arranging exchanges between American and Saudi institutions. I am also continuing doing interfaith dialogue with individuals I met, including a lengthy dialogue with Rebecca K. Mays, a devoted Christian Quaker. An excerpt of our correspondence follows.

Dear Fahad,

I would very much appreciate if you would send me the reference you mentioned at our meeting in Washington, D.C. It was a reference from the Qur'an about how tears will be shed when one recognizes salvation.

Looking forward to hearing from you,

Rebecca

Dear Rebecca,

As for the verses from the Qur'an about tears for those Christians who recognize the truth, please find it below. It is in chapter (5 *al-Maeda*) "The Table," verses 82-85.

(5: 82) Strongest among men in enmity to the believers wilt thou find the Jews and Pagans; and nearest among them in love to the believers wilt thou find those who say, "We are Christians": because amongst these are men devoted to learning and men who have renounced the world, and they are not arrogant.

(5: 83) And when they listen to the revelation received by the Messenger, thou wilt see their eyes overflowing with tears, for they recognize the truth: they pray: "Our Lord! we believe; write us down among the witnesses.

(5: 84) What cause can we have not to believe in Allah and the truth which has come to us, seeing that we long for our Lord to admit us to the company of the righteous?"

(5: 85) And for this their prayer hath Allah rewarded them with gardens, with rivers flowing underneath, their eternal home. Such is the recompense of those who do good.

(5: 86) But those who reject Faith and belie our Signs, they shall be companions of Hell-fire.

May God rejoin us in His Paradise.

Thanks Rebecca for asking me about the above verses.

Hi Fahad,

When I read these verses you have sent, I wonder how did you interpret my tears? Did you think I was finding my salvation in Islam? When you recognized the tears, you used the word "shocking." Why?

All best,

Rebecca

Dear Rebecca,

Here are three issues:

About our conversation at the Catholic University of America while we were getting our lunch, which I do remember vividly. Here are my comments.

Before I explain what I meant, I would rather give you my opinion or understanding of Christianity as a religion. I believe that God has sent prophets and messengers to people to guide them about how to live on this Earth until they go back to their original eternal home, Heaven. If they obey God's rules, which are revealed through his prophets and messengers, then they will be saved; otherwise, they will be punished based on their bad deeds; then they will be cleared from their sins and finally will go to Heaven.

So, many prophets were sent down, until Jesus came, who was different, as he was the word of God. Instead of the scrolls which were given to Moses or the Qur'an orally revealed to Muhammad as the word of God, Jesus was himself the word of God. So for Christians, the deeds and actions of Jesus represent God's will. But somehow Christians believe that Jesus, the Holy Spirit and God are one. Other concepts began to emerge in Christian belief such as salvation, obedience, redemption, etc. Then God sent a new prophet to get people back to the same teachings that He revealed to Moses and Jesus but with corrections to the Christian understanding of those concepts. When Muhammad came with the Qur'an to elaborate these issues, some Christians, those who come with open mind and heart and look deeply to what God has revealed to them in Qur'an, will recognize the truth of what Muhammad has brought as a message and their tears will flow.

When you told me about your belief in Salvation and that when you had your first child you could not believe your daughter would go to Hellfire without being first saved, I told you that this is the same belief I have. Your tears came and so I thought it is because of the truth you recognized. That's all, and I would like to hear from you whether my understanding is accurate and what would you say about the flowing tears.

I will get back to you with the verse you asked me about next time, I gotta go now.

Dear Fahad,

I appreciate your explanation of your faith. When reading about Wahhabism, I am most struck by the concept of "tawhid" or the "unity of God." I once received a powerful dream filled with Light in which I was commanded to seek Union with God . . . That command more than anything else has me interested in the dialogue work. I want to understand through people's experiences how God's unity will come into reality.

When we agreed on a child's innocence I wept not just because of the agreement but because I sensed the presence of what I call the Holy Spirit. This presence was increasing our understanding more through a felt sense than through words. This felt sense of God was for me an experience of God's unity establishing understanding between us. I became a Quaker in part because we do not see heaven and hell as a life after this one; rather, we see heaven and hell in how we choose to live our lives on earth now. Our responsibility as humans is to create heaven on earth, here and now through establishing justice, harmony, and peace. I felt we were doing that work and that God was blessing it.

I love gardens. I love the infinite possibility of forms. Sometimes I smile, imagining God just having a playful time thinking, "Now what shape and color might I try to express this beauty of the unity of this created order." And then I remind myself not to project onto God what I cannot know. What I can know are moments when we are to be humble before the salvific power of the One we worship, however differently we may worship. Fahad, I am privileged to have shared the tears of joy in recognizing the One who makes dialogue worth trying. I pray for your continued good work and mine so that lives will not be lost over the differences between our two faith traditions.

Peace and Love to you at this my family's most holy Christmastide,

Rebecca

. .. .

DAY EIGHTY NINE :: WEDNESDAY
DECEMBER 10, 2008
"I think there is something, more important than believing: Action! The world is full of dreamers, there aren't enough who will move ahead and begin to take concrete steps to actualize their vision."

— W. Clement Stone, American author, (1902-2002)

T he ICAP program and the new dialogues with friends in the U.S. have inspired me to initiate the birth of the Western Studies Institute (WSI). The Mission of WSI is to encourage mutual understanding and cooperation between the Islamic and Western worlds with the following activities.

Education: To educate peoples of the Islamic World about western humanities and sciences.

Research: To foster research on western humanities and sciences as these apply to the Islamic World.

Translation: To foster the translation of appropriate material into languages of the Islamic World.

Publication: To foster the publication of original works, translations, periodicals, etc.

Cultural Exchanges: To foster interreligious and intercultural events and activities.

*My Fulbright Visiting Scholars group gathered for a
photo at the State Department in Washington, D.C.*

There are hundreds of centers and institutes on Orientalism, or Arabic or Eastern
or Islamic Studies etc. but as far as I know there is none that focuses on Western
Studies. I have been eager to establish such an institute and to be a pioneer from
the East who initiates this great mission. Affiliated with this institute, I have also
established the *Journal of Western Studies (JWS)*. The aim of *JWS* is to promote the
exchange of information and knowledge among researchers around the globe
in general, and among Arabic-English speaking practitioners, and educators in
particular. It is a bilingual, peer-reviewed publication. I pray for continued guidance
and support for this project.

. . ..

DAY NINETY :: THURSDAY
DECEMBER 11, 2008

"Wise are those who learn that the bottom line doesn't always have to be their top priority."

— William Arthur Ward, American author, (1921-1994)

The feeling I have ending my journey and leaving my readers is different than the
feeling I had in the beginning of writing this journey. The hesitation I felt at the
beginning was mixed with an anxious yet enthusiastic excitement; a challenging
feeling motivated by curiosity. Now, I am hesitant to stop writing, feeling attached to
many people in this book with whom I exchanged knowledge and shared great memories.
My hesitation comes also from my wanting to write more for those who have never
explored America, or for those who have been there but saw it with different eyes and
minds. I hope my perspectives can help make vivid the best of America.

I have focused on four main categories with many entries in each. The first category
is about the major events, figures, and movements in the American history. The second
is about American institutions and political parties. The third is about the modern
American culture including pop culture, sport and the many personalities of American.
The fourth is about the religious diversity in America, particularly Judaism, Christianity
and Islam.

I have felt obliged to write this book. Having spent four years in America, from
July 1997 until July 2001, during which I visited over thirty states. I could tell the vast
differences between that time and these three months as a Fulbright Visiting Scholar
in 2008. The tragic events of 9-11 (when members of an Islamic radical movement
attacked NYC) had increased the distance between the American and Muslim peoples,
especially those of Saudi Arabia. I felt obligated to write, to try and describe my interest
in America in a way that is accessible to Saudis and other Muslims. I want as well for
Americans to know how I and others understand them. I want to decrease the distance
that has happened and to make the journeys of prayer and travel safe and well-informed.

Notes

Notes

Fahad A. Alhomoudi, Ph.D.

Fahad Alhomoudi was born in Riyadh, Saudi Arabia, where he gained a B.A. in Islamic Studies, an M.A. from Imam Muhammad bin Saud Islamic University in Protecting the Environment and Natural Sources, and a Ph.D. in Islamic Studies from McGill University, Montreal, Canada. He works at Imam University as Vice Dean of Academic Research and serves Princess Nora bint Abdu Rahman University as a consultant for the Rector.

As a Fulbright Visiting Scholar to the U.S. in 2008, Fahad has engaged in extensive Intercultural/Interfaith Dialogue initiatives, including the establishment of the Western Studies Institute which he founded in 2009. The first of its kind, this Institute will address the Arab audience to help reframe prejudices between the Arab and Western worlds. Dr. Alhomoudi's publications include: *Protecting the Environment and the Natural Sources in Islamic Law* (Riyadh: Ishbilia Publishing, 2002); *On the Common-Link Theory: Remapping Western Theories on Islamic Law* (Germany: Vdm Verlag Dr. Muller Aktiengesellschaft & Co. Kg, 2008); and "Islamic Law and the Modern State: Conflict or Co-existence?" in the volume of proceedings for the Center for American Studies and Research (Beirut: American University of Beirut, 2008).

Currently, Dr. Alhomoudi is working in Riyadh on his new project: an encyclopaedia of the writings of western travelers to the Arabian Peninsula between 1850-1950.

The author encourages correspondence at *homoudi@gmail.com*.